UWAH PETERDAMIAN UCHE

THE NATURE OF MAN

(Body, Soul & Spirit)

AuthorHouse™ UK
1663 Liberty Drive
Bloomington, IN 47403 USA
www.authorhouse.co.uk
UK TFN: 0800 0148641 (Toll Free inside the UK)
UK Local: 02036 956322 (+44 20 3695 6322 from outside the UK)

Because of the dynamic nature of the Internet, any web addresses or links contained in this book may have changed since publication and may no longer be valid. The views expressed in this work are solely those of the author and do not necessarily reflect the views of the publisher, and the publisher hereby disclaims any responsibility for them.

Any people depicted in stock imagery provided by Getty Images are models, and such images are being used for illustrative purposes only. Certain stock imagery © Getty Images.

This book is printed on acid-free paper.

ISBN: 979-8-8230-8464-2 (sc)
979-8-8230-8465-9 (e)

Library of Congress Control Number: 2023917382

Print information available on the last page.

Published by AuthorHouse 10/12/2023

authorHOUSE®

DEDICATION

This book is dedicated to every SPIRIT-MAN serving God in truth and spirit.

ACKNOWLEDGEMENTS

I sincerely wish to acknowledge my indebtedness to the Supreme Being, Abba Father, the Almighty God who elevated my spirit to understand these revelations by the power of the Holy Ghost to articulate this piece of information. My profound gratitude goes to my brother and man of God, Rev. Fr. Prof. I. E. Uwah, for his contributions, support and guidance to spiritual matters and his precise role in the success of this project.

My profound thanks to my most cherished wife and children and my family members, who have supported my career and pursuits in life one way or the other. To them, I am grateful.

Finally, to my mum and dad, I will forever love and appreciate you because, without you, there is no me. Gratitude forever!

CONTENTS

FOREWORD

The desire to save mankind from sin, death and eternal damnation is the sole purpose for which Jesus Christ, the only son of God undertook crucifixion on the cross, died and was buried and resurrected on the third day. His journey from heaven to earth was a tedious one, but because he placed a high premium on the salvation of man, he did not shrink away from undertaking such a route that would lead to his death to bring humanity back to God after the fall of Adam and Eve. The work of Jesus does not only show his love and compassion for all human beings but also signals his Divine intention for all to embrace the sanctity of life as to be counted as his co-heirs to the kingdom of God. The apostles continued this trajectory of saving souls and like them, many churches in our time are still engaged in ringing the bell of invitation to the banquet hall of the master. This, too, is the course Mr. Peterdamian Uche Uwah has taken up in his book, *The Nature of Man*.

Written in simple flowing English language, *The Nature of Man* is a work dedicated to guiding those interested in living up to their spiritual calling. The author believes that man is called to be spiritual or to use his construction, man is a spirit in human flesh. His effort in explicating the true nature of man as not merely mundane and secular yielded to his using mathematical formulas to prove man to be a higher being far from the limitations of nature. *The Nature of Man,* therefore, is a book written to awaken in its readers the urgency of the times which is becoming conscious of the spiritual nature granted them by God from the beginning since all mankind do participate in the being of God by having his breath in them and knowing his will for mankind's salvation. It is a book interlaced with biblical quotations to convince readers of the veracity of the powers of the Holy Spirit if only man can dwell in the word of God and abide by its kingdom principles. In this book, the author argues that living carnally is very dangerous because it leads to doom. Among the panaceas he recommends for remaining afloat the dangers of the world are prayer, meditation, and the word of God.

The Nature of Man is logically equipped to enlighten its readers on how to grow by facing God consciously and not allow themselves to be dragged down by the forces of darkness operating across the length and breadth of the world in which man inhabits. To take up *The Nature of Man* and not read is a disservice to the soul because it is a book written with the view that by consuming its treasures man can grow from who one is to where God wants him to be. It should be seen as a vade mecum for spiritual conversion and everyday living in the Lord. It is a well-packaged, simple document infused with spiritual grenades for convinced change makers. In it, Mr. Uche PD Uwah presents a believer's manifesto for a step-by-step journey to higher realms of the spirit. This work will serve not only the needs of individual souls but also those of groups and sodalities in the Church wishing to grow by learning the word of God and appreciating how special they are in the sight of their maker. I recommend it for use by all desiring to walk consciously in the presence of God and by so doing worship him in spirit and truth. While congratulating the author for the contributions his book makes to the spiritual growth of man, I pray that God blesses all who would savour the treasures deposited in the book and by so doing grow in the knowledge of God and man as to appreciate their value in him who has called them to higher heights as spiritual beings. Enjoy it!

Rev. Fr. Prof. I. E. Uwah
University of Port Harcourt

PREFACE

Right through the years, when I started knowing things about God, having been tormented spiritually because of ignorance, I was graciously delivered in 1997 and became born-again. With great zeal, I made fasting and prayer my coat of arms; meditation and quiet times became the order of the day. With the gift of the word of Knowledge (Rhema) from God Almighty and the logos of the WORD, I realized why God had taken me far and wide to learn spiritual things. He taught me things I should know, instigating me to ask myself questions…who am I? God began to lift my spirit in perceiving who I am. He began to lift my spirit in perceiving who I am and the place he has given man in the world. My faith grew, and I came to a new understanding that man is highly positioned by the supreme being as next to God in the order of hierarchy. – Man, next to God in the order of hierarchy.

Sequel to this understating, having seen that man has lost his dignity, it perturbs me tremendously to let 'men' know who they are. My consciousness of this fact made me raise questions about why most people do not yet know the will of God concerning them. I was always getting one scriptural answer, which was like a revelation on the poverty of the souls of those rescued. It is a confession of a sort made by Prophet Hosea,

"My people are destroyed for lack of knowledge" - Hosea 4:6

The truth of this calls for pity as much as it is a call for human beings to seek remedy in the form of salvation from ignorance which only Jesus, Divine illumination, can give. Since every human being is unique (remarkable), there is a need for no one to disappoint the expectations of living fully and faithfully. As the word of God tells us, man is not meant to die; in; him is eternal life, the life of God.

Man is unique (remarkable). He (man) is the perfect reflection of the nature of God, his nature and consciousness. He is a spirit, magnified to have a living soul in situ in the body. **(1 Thessalonians 5:23)**. Man is not meant to die and cannot die; in Him is eternal life, the life of God. **(1 John 5:13b).**

Man has willpower. Yes, that is, the dynamic ability to act and to cause changes, to control both inanimate and animate objects, and they will obey him. The Holy Spirit is still working to teach man all things. The question is: Why should man behave and die like an animal? I repeat, why should man behave and die like an animal? - when God had warned all in the book of Psalms by saying thus:

"I have said, ye are gods, and all of you are children of the most High.

-Psalms 82:6

The previous verse of this Psalm 82 chapter in the fifth verse, declares:

"They know not, neither will they understand; they walk on in the darkness, All the foundations of the earth are out, of course."

-Psalm 82:5

The thrust of this book is that human beings should wake up from their slumber and discover who they are to recover their lost glory. Humanity is on a journey to perfection. God is a spirit, angels are spirit beings, and man is a spirit. What is born of spirit is also spirit. Man is a little God. The only difference between the unseen spirit and man is that man was highly magnified to dwell in a body. He possesses two natures: human and divine nature.

Human nature, in the sense that he dwells in a body and divine nature because man is a spirit. Here lies the top secret, which Jesus exposes to us. Meanwhile, when a prince behaves like a mere servant, it is an 'evil' under the sun, a mystery of iniquity. In earnest, this work will direct man (you and I) to know the son of whom we are and then should we respect ourselves. We are even higher than the angels. Son of man, recall! The word of God declares this Divine vision when, it is asked in the book of Hebrew:

"Are they not all ministering spirits, sent forth to minister for them who shall be heirs of salvation?"

Hebrews 1:14

I call on all to read through the pages and fire up to merit salvation (liberation of soul and mind), which Jesus gives to all, free of charge. Welcome to knowing yourself more and becoming spirit-led. It is a spiritual journey, and I am happy to have you onboard. Let's go!

INTRODUCTION

"But one in a certain place testified saying, what is <u>man</u>, that thou art mindful of him? Or the son of man, that thou visitest him? Thou madest him a little lower than the angels, thou crownest him with glory and honour, and didst set him over the works of thy hands. Thou hadst put <u>all things</u> in subjection under his feet. For in that, he put all in subjection under him; he left nothing that is not put under him. But we see Jesus, who was made a little lower than the angels for the suffering of death, crowned with glory and honour, that he, by the grace of God, should taste death for every man".

Hebrews 2:6-9 KJV

Man is not ordinary in the sight of God. God loves man unconditionally and clothed him with honour and glory. Man, indeed, is highly magnified.

From the day God created man, he thought about it and gave it a pause before he released his best. Man is the best 'thing' God could have ever created. That is why he rested after creating man. He (God) was pleased with himself and concluded that he was good and rested. God did not hesitate to make man the general overseer of all his creation. The only thing man can do is acknowledge his place in God's Divine plan and vision. Knowing it and working with God is living a purposeful life, which all men are called to have.

According to the man of God, Doctor Myles Munroe, *"the greatest tragedy on planet earth is not death, but a life without purpose".* Man does not know whom and who he is. He could not recognise himself. Man does not know who he is if he lives without a purpose. He can be said not to recognize himself or squarely not to be conscious of his dignity. When a man loses his Divine-given spirit, his identity is shattered, and he can be said to have been 'ichabodised', that is, without his glory as a child of God. This glory can only be restored in Christ, and great thanks to him, our Lord Jesus, for coming to restore human beings to their lost glory and to his dignity. The Bible tells us that 'man' was made in God's image, consciousness, and likeness. 'Man' ought to know that he represents God on earth. He ought to reason like God, act like God and represent God. In this book, **"THE NATURE OF MAN",** I will delineate God's nature of man and how man is more than ordinary. You and I, as human beings, are Divinely packaged. We are special to God. We are highly exalted not by degrees and titles but by God, who created us in his image, which is supernatural and made his son, Jesus Christ, to be our saviour and our brother. Man, therefore, and that is who you are, is a spirit. You are unique. You are born to be eternal and to manifest Divine powers because you have the spirit of God alive in you. This is what we will guide you to appreciate here as we look at the nature of man in the first chapter to foreground an overview. This is what the quotation cited at the beginning of this introductory page helps us understand by letting us know that we spend time taking care of ourselves. We are important to him. He purchases us with the blood of his only son, a sacrifice that is not cheap by any standard. He created us, a little less than the angels ministering to him in heaven and bequeathed his glory on us as lovely works of his choice. God in choosing us has also given up everything for our use and care, and all other creatures are under our rule. Does this not inform us of the place of glory that man occupies? Yes, that is it: The nature of man is so highly placed, and we are not qualified to downplay its dignity!

I am going to elaborate on the following questions on man,

- Is he a spirit?
- Does he have a living soul that dwells in the body?
- Does he acquire willpower from God?
- What makes him unique, and what is man?

Chapter ONE

THE NATURE OF MAN: AN OVERVIEW

Amazingly, it is incredible that many people in our world today cannot defend their status and magnanimity because they lack definition.

Everything in life has a definition, yet man cannot define himself because he lost his identity long ago. This is pathetic.

Man's life on earth is of a short time, and he needs to enjoy the splendour of honour and glory deposited in him by his creator. Man cannot attain this without understanding who he is.

MAN

Of all God's creations, man's being is a mystery; as Gabriel Marcel, the existentialist philosopher, says, He (man) stands at the crossroads of creation. Above and around him are spirits and angels, in corporal beings, yet he is more magnified than them. Man has something of the material and something of the spiritual. He is what we call a rational being. His being makes demands on him, which must satisfy his body, spirit, and soul – intellectual parts.

Invariably, the nature of man falls under three (3) categories:

→ Man lives in a physical BODY.

→ He has a living SOUL and

→ He is a SPIRIT   **-1 Thessalonians 5:23**

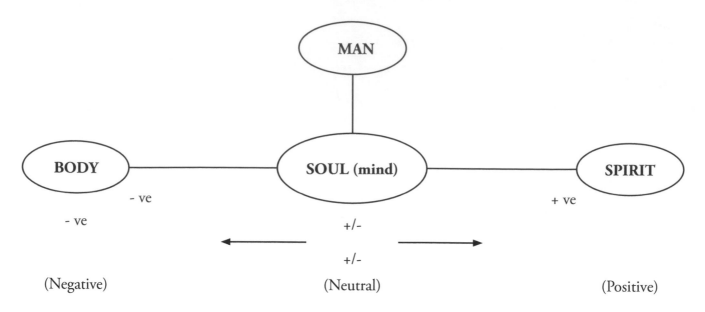

(Negative)   (Neutral)   (Positive)

The diagram above depicts the existence of man in the consciousness of divinity (spirit), carnality (body), and the flexibility of the soul (mind) to the objective consciousness (-ve) or the subjective consciousness (+ve). These will be explained later in this book.

Man's personality could be interpreted from the fundamentals, from the creation of the world, by the Almighty God, who is the All and All, the universal consciousness; from whom everything that is, is in him; and emanated from him. Our references could be taken from Genesis, chapters 1 and 2.

> **"And God said, let us make man in our image, after our likeness . . . so**
> **God created man in his image, in the image of God, He created him."**
>
> **-Genesis 1:26,**
>
> **"And the Lord God formed man out of the dust of the ground and**
> **breathed into his nostrils, the breath of life, and man became a <u>living soul.</u>"**
>
> **-Genesis 2:7**

The biblical text above reveals that God formed man in his image. The source of life (living soul) is God. In this context, the word "image" displays an essence of being; when I said essence, I meant all that makes a thing, what it is.

Fundamentally, man's personality was void-*ab initio* until something extraordinarily strategic occurred. God consciously breathed his spirit into man's being via his nostrils; this breath from God is the breath of life that is eternal, which makes 'man' a living and functional being – A LIVING SOUL.

There is no complete man without breathing in the spirit; instead, a dust formed from the earth that was inactive and mortal.

When God breathed into the nostrils of the to-be-man, I repeat, something extraordinary happened. He (God) deposited a "GOD-LIKE" consciousness into man's body system, which is the soul, that was diffused using a vibration force, and the spirit of God acted as a medium.

In other words, God sent his spirit into the being of man, which dwells in man and enables man to become a living soul.

Note: The spirit of God, the Holy Spirit, is God's acting medium of execution.

"Thou sendest forth thy spirit; they are created, and thou renewest the face of the earth."

- Psalm 104:30 (KJV)

Hold on, get it clearly, the bible says in Saint John's gospel, chapter 4, verse 24. . . **God is a spirit** . . ., and in the calendar and timetable of God, it pleased Him to make man in his image, nature, and consciousness (**Genesis1:26**). Please recall that when God was creating the universe, He commanded things to come out from its source, for example, God commanded the sea to give yield to fish, sea animals, etc... This is the reason why these inhabitants could not survive outside their source and even when they die, return to their source. Such principle is also applied to the land's trees, herbs, shrubs, and beasts because their source is the Earth (dust). Hence, when they die, they return to their source. This means that every life has a source.

However, if a man becomes a living – soul by breathing in from God, that means that man's source of life is GOD. Do not blink; come with me, you will agree that a mango tree will yield mango fruit, an orange tree will surely yield orange fruit, and a maize stem will yield cob of maize grains. If that is the case, what is born of the spirit is spirit. This suggests that man is a spirit.

The Extraordinary strategic event occurred when God breathed into man's nostrils. He released and deposited his spirit into the already-formed dust, the to-be-man, the mortal man. Nevertheless, it is the spirit of God that quickens. This spirit from God transformed the immortal man and quickened and as well domiciled in him. The Bible bears witness to this in Romans 8:11; please read this carefully.

"But if the Spirit of Him that raised Jesus from the dead dwells in you, He that raised Christ from the dead will also quicken (revitalize) your mortal bodies by his spirit that dwelleth in you."

Romans 8:11

Listen carefully!

The God-like consciousness he deposited in us could have been worthless if he did not give us his spirit to "KICK-START" it in us, making us living souls.

Promptly, God made man a living soul, even by allowing his spirit to dwell in us. The spirit of God quickens; it dwells in the physical body and quickens the soul; teaching, the spirit of man (because automatically man is a spirit) makes man unique amongst God's creations.

What a glory! The spirit of God dwells in the human person's existence and personality. It is real. There is no doubt about all this.

> **"Know ye not that; ye are the temple of God,**
> **and the spirit of God dwelleth in you."**
>
> **I Corinthians 3:16**

In earnest, the nature of man is the image of God. He (man) is living in a physical body, having a quickened living soul, and he is a spirit. This makes 'man' a classical reflection of the perfection of God's image and nature. Man is so elevated that even God testified in his words through the voice of His psalmist testifying in Psalm 82.

> **"I have said, ye are gods, and all of you are children of the most High."**
>
> **- Psalm 82:6**

- THE SPIRIT OF GOD IN MAN –

The spirit of God, dwelling in man, is to assist the spirit of man, or rather to assist man (because man automatically is a spirit), to attain spiritual things. He directs man's spirit or rather the spirit man, teaching him, even unto showing him things to come.

This is one reason why spiritual men of God (men whom the Holy Spirit of God is leading) are one step ahead of ordinary men (any man living in carnality). When 'man' has fellowship with the spirit of God and communes with the spirit, He (the spirit) teaches man about heavenly things (word of knowledge); He shows man things to do and to know (vision) and things to come (revelation), etc.

Being the dynamic executor of the word of God to cause changes, if man (a spirit man) makes a prayer, the Holy Spirit channels it to God. He intercedes for us, assuming the office of a mediator between God and man (**Romans 8:26-27**). This same Holy Spirit is the Christ, the "Word", now in spirit, who bears the name JESUS in flesh, blood, and water. Do not marvel at this; here lies a mystery, and it takes a revelation to know God out of conviction, not conversion. The explanation goes forth as follows . . . read below,

-CHRIST IN MAN-

Jesus told Nicodemus that he must be born again to inherit the Kingdom of God.

Born-again extends beyond the flesh; it deals with more of the spirit. We are talking about spiritual matters because we are spirits. Christ cannot be in man in the form of flesh, never, but rather in spirit form.

Taking it from the first principles, "Christ the word" takes a significant position in the creation of the universe. The Bible testifies in the first chapter of the gospel of St John about the divinity of Christ the Word, the Existence of Christ the Jesus on planet Earth, and his personality in the life of man today as Christ the Holy Spirit. Forget about theology and philosophy, and do not allow religious spirit to overwhelm you; let's see what God declares in his word.

"In the beginning was the WORD, and the word was with God,
and the WORD was GOD. The same was at the beginning with God.
He made all things, and without him was not
anything made, that was made".

- **John 1: 1-3**

In another position of the bible, the chapter reveals,

"Thou sendest forth thy spirit; they are created,
and thou renewest the face of the earth."

-Psalm 104:30

The first biblical text reveals that God sent his "word", and the universe was created. Hence, classifying the "word, as the chief executive officer (C.E.O.) in the manufacturing company of God. On the other hand, in the second biblical text, the CEO of God's Manufacturing Company is classified as the spirit. These two texts show that the word and the spirit are the same. The "word" is the "spirit", and the "spirit" is the word. Watch this-

"And take the helmet of salvation, and the sword of the spirit,
which is the word of God."

-Ephesians 6:17

Jesus, in one of his teachings to his disciples, emphasizes,

"The words I speak to you, they are spirit, and they are life (John 6:63)."

In other words, the word of God is spirit, and the spirit is the word. The spirit quickens the word and makes it come alive.

Progressing from Chapter One of the gospel of St. John, the bible declares in the fourteenth verse . . .

"And the <u>word was made flesh</u> and dwelleth among us.
(And we beheld his glory, the glory as the only begotten of the father),
full of grace and truth".

-John 1:14

This word made flesh is the same Jesus.

What makes this same "WORD", the executive CEO of God, the spirit that creates things from the beginning, transcended from his glorious and prestigious abode and was made flesh, and dwelleth among the apostles, and they beheld his glory? A question one may ask. The explanation for these occurrences should be termed a "chain reaction". However, I will try to summarize it.

It pains God to see man, whom he loves so much (John **3: 16**), disobeying him by giving heed to Satan. Satan, the Devil, hoodwinks man by convincing him to do what God has forewarned them (Adam and Eve) to desist from. So, man lost his position in the Garden of Eden (Place of authority). Satan, the Leviathan, the Lucifer, indirectly overthrows man from his God-given position in life; the first *coup de tat* originally happened in the Garden of Eden. Satan snatched away from man the government that God had entrusted into man's hand to occupy, subdue, rule, and oversee all his creations. Because the bible says (whom you yield yourself to, such have you become a servant to), this is incredible; Man becomes an enslaved person in the hands of Satan. Things that are supposed not to come into existence.

Initially, man does not struggle to eat. There was no death. Death would have been a stranger to man to life infinity. Sickness was imposed on man by Satan. Hatred, killings, hunger, afflictions, and evil were introduced into man's life. Pain and anguish became the order of the day from the government of Satan.

As we all know, before any rebel soldiers engage in war, they look for or spy on loopholes and weak point zones of their attackers, which draws a strategic map for the mission. Satan did not forget all these; hence, he outlined his motto,

"STEAL, KILL & DESTROY" (**John 10; 10**). This is the motto of Satan to Humanity. Unaware to Satan, this same "WORD" that could not rest until all creation was perfected agreed with God for him to manifest as flesh to save man. Out of this resolution, the "WORD", which is Christ, comes to planet Earth to save humanity from the torment and torture of Satan. Jesus, the world-made flesh, became the human manifestation of the heavenly Christ, the word of God.

"For God so loved the world, that he gave his only begotten son,
that whosoever believeth in him should not perish,
but having everlasting life."

-John 3:16

And Jesus was born (**John 1:14**). The bible bearing witness to this says,

"For this purpose, the son of God was manifested
that He might destroy the works of the devil."

- John 3:8

No wonder Satan was not relaxed; when he heard about Jesus coming into the world, he disturbed Joseph to put away Mary, his betrothed (wife) or call for abortion, deceiving him that Mary had gone out to sleep with another man, but God intervened. Unrelenting, he (Satan) tormented Herod, forcing him to kill all the children born in the Land from two (2) years and under. What a genocide! All these happened to terminate the critical assignment Christ came to do. As if that was not enough, he tempted Him three times in the wilderness. But Jesus conquered all these. When Jesus started his ministry, He graciously informed us why the Father had sent him.

And He said,

"The thief (Satan) cometh not but for to steal,
Kill and destroy. I have come that they might have life
and have it more abundantly."

-John 10:10 KJV

When the actual time for the assignment came to pass, Jesus strategically died, willingly as planned, and descended into Hades. In Hades, Jesus confronted Satan face to face, defeated him and released man from the bondage of Satan and sin and death. He made an open show of Satan and his cohorts.

"And having spoiled principality and powers,
He made a shew of them openly, triumphing over them."

-Colossians 2:15

Jesus defeated Satan, collected the power, and restored it to man. And Jesus emphatically declared. . .

"All power is given unto me both in heaven and on earth."

-Mathew 28:18

And he released it to man, saying, **"I give it to you to thread upon serpents and scorpions and to thread upon the powers of the enemy (Satan,) and nothing shall by any means hurt you" (Luke 10:19).** He further commissioned man, saying "**whatsoever you bind on planet Earth is bound in heaven and whatever you lose is loosed in heaven" (Mathew 18:18).**

The assignment has partly been accomplished. And since it is the time for Jesus to go to the Father, he promised man to be with him always because of the love he got for man (**John 15:13).** He said to Man, "**It is so expedient that I go to the father. . ." (John 14:1**)

So that wherever He is, there we will be also. He promised man to ask his father, Papa God, to give the man another comforter. This is to say, He will ask his father (intercede) to send his word (Note: Whatsoever that GOD demands, He only sends his word), and his word is Jesus. In other words, he will ask the father to give him another assignment to comfort man, not only for a while but permanently. Christ died, resurrected and is with God reigning with him, sitting at the right hand of God. This means that as Christ died, He restored man to his glory and dignity, now man sitting at the right hand of God reigning with Christ (**John 14:1-3**). (Note: This is a metaphorical statement). And so, for the love he had with and for man, He requested from the Father to dwell in man and comfort him always.

"And I will pray the Father, and he shall give you another comforter,
that he may abide with you forever.
Even the spirit of truth... I will not leave you comfortless,
I will come to you."

-John 14:16, 17&18

This is a mystery and calls for understanding. Jesus knows the modus operandi of God. God sends his "WORD", and the Holy Spirit of God has always quickened this word. This is to say that the Word is the Spirit, and the Spirit is the Word.

In other words, the spirit will **not** quicken the "word" to become flesh this time; instead, the spirit will quicken the "word" of God to be released by God; it is holy and being quickened is the holy spirit. Therefore, the "word" JESUS manifested in the flesh dwelling among the people will be the Holy Spirit (the word) manifested in the spirit dwelling inside man.

Hence, the word and the spirit, quickened to be in the full manifestation of the spirit, become one spirit and dwell in man to comfort him forever. Sincerely speaking, God sent his "word", and it becomes flesh, which is JESUS, to save humanity.

"There is no name given under the heaven,
among men to save mankind, except that name JESUS."

Invariably, in this second assignment to comfort man, God sent his "word" to become spirit, to inspire man. This "word" being sent becomes the Holy Spirit.

> **"And he that keepeth his commandment dwelleth in him, and he in him.**
> **And at this moment, we know that he abideth in us, by the Spirit**
> **which he hath given us".** 1 John 3:24 KJV

(Note: The Holy Spirit manifested after Jesus died and ascended into the heavens).

CHRIST THE WORD   *SPIRIT   JESUS
                                     ⎯⎯⎯→
                                      FLESH

CHRIST THE WORD   *SPIRIT   HOLY SPIRIT
                                       ⎯⎯⎯→
                                       SPIRIT

The *spirit here acts as a catalyst (biologically speaking), which quickens a substance's chemical reaction rate. The spirit * quickens.

One of my best friends, who understood this mystery as I do, stated it clearly to the Colossians of the early church of Christ. He said this had been a mystery for years, but God has graciously revealed the secret of this mystery to us all now, which is this.

'CHRIST THE WORD' IN YOU, BEARING THE NAME, HOLY SPIRIT

When Christ was on planet Earth, he dwelt among them (apostles, disciples), etc.; when he resurrected, he lives in us (GLORY!).

> **"Even the mystery which hath been hidden from ages and generations,**
> **but now is made manifest to his saints.**
> **To whom God would make known what are the riches of the glory**
> **of this mystery among the Gentiles, which is, <u>Christ in you, the hope of glory.</u>"**
> **-Colossians 1:26-27**

'Man' was restored to his creator, given power, and was glorified. As a man, when God looks at you, He no longer sees you, He sees Christ in the form of the Holy Spirit in YOU. This is amazing. The Holy Spirit is everywhere.

> **"You are of God, little children and have overcome them,**
> **Because greater is he that is in you than he that is in the world."**
> **- John 4:4**

Chapter TWO

MAN: AN ETERNAL SPIRIT

**"And the very God of peace sanctify you wholly, and I pray God,
your whole <u>spirit</u> and <u>soul</u> and <u>body</u> be preserved
blameless unto the coming of our LORD JESUS CHRIST."**

1 Thessalonians 5:23

In Chapter 1, I have carefully mentioned the nature of man into three (3) categories of

- Spirit
- Soul
- Body

Man is a spirit. He has a soul (LIVING SOUL) and a physical body. Man as a spirit–being is made in the image of GOD. The Bible says in the gospel of Saint John chapter 4, verse 24, that GOD is a spirit, and man being created in God's image, likeness, and nature is, no doubt, a spirit.

Man is an eternal being, then a sense that when our physical body, which is our earthly house, becomes too old for the Spirit-man to continue to dwell further or is being destroyed, the spirit lives on eternally. Man is not meant to die; He (man) is eternal and cannot die.

Knowing fully well that you disagree with that, let us examine together, in the spirit of brotherhood, what the BIBLE says about Man. Here we go . . .

At this periphery, permit me to use the keywords "*Outward man*" and "*Inward man*" to represent the physical body and the spirit man (-the real man), respectively. Before I go further in explaining the idea of man being eternal, I wish to recall the word of St JOHN in his understanding of man . . . He says:

**"You are of GOD, little children and have overcome them.
Because <u>greater is he that is in you</u> than he that is in the world".**

-1 John 4:4

In this physical body dwells more extraordinary beings – the spirit of God (Holy Ghost) and the spirit of man – (inward-man). God's Eternal and Immortal Spirit makes His abode in the temple of God. And as the spirit-man (inward man) fellowships with HIM (Holy Ghost), He (Holy Ghost) teaches the inward man the Kingdom principles. He reveals, teaches, comforts, exhorts, admonishes, and guides the inward man unto perfection. Everyone who passes through existence encounters challenges, and those who conquer them do so in the spirit. John refers to this when he says, 'You have overcome them'. Those who are victorious are of God. They lived life in respect of God's wishes for them. They subdued their bodies. They disciplined the flesh. They did not live according to the dictates of the world. They lived by serving God in spirit and in truth.

The outward man (physical body) could die, decay and rot away to the Earth; the spirit man sojourns into the spiritual realm, where it lives eternally.

WHAT THEN HAPPENS TO THE SPIRIT –MAN?

A question one may ask. I will answer this question by illustrating some critical points from the epistle of St. Paul, who, out of revelation, knew the truth of man's personality.

Talking to the church in Philippians, he says,

> **'For I am in a strait betwixt two,**
> **having a desire to depart and to be with Christ, which is far better,**
> **nevertheless, to abide in the flesh is more needful for you.**
> **-Philippians 1:23, 24**

In other words, our brother Paul said that if he remains in the physical body, it will be profitable to the Philippians church as he will continue ministering the word of God. Instead, for him to depart out of his physical body and sojourn, Christ will be far better to do so. He acknowledges the secret of his being that he never dies; he could only be departing out of the physical body. He is an eternal spirit.

Meanwhile, I would like to state that GOD owns our life (spirit, soul & body) **Psalm 24:1**; once someone's spirit departs from the physical body (outward man), he returns to the supreme GOD and presents himself. HERE IS THE JUDGMENT! (**Luke 16:19-31**).

GOD who is perfect and holy, and does not behold iniquity, and has declared that he demands **a church without wrinkle, a church without blemish, a church without spot**, *(Eph 5:27),* will only accept an upright spirit-man (inward man). On the other hand (vice-versa), if the spirit man is not upright, he will be cast into the lake of fire, where he will suffer, with the gnashing of teeth forever and ever. However, if he (spirit-man) is upright, for unto him is joy in the kingdom of GOD forever – **Paradise!**

Paradise could be said to be the earthly Garden of Eden (in Absentia), where man lost or was driven away because of the sin of Adam & Eve. Hence, Jesus came to restore us to paradise, where there is supreme bliss and abundance of life.

"The enemy came to steal, kill and destroy;
but I came to give them life in abundance, the Kingdom of God."

-John 10:10

Lord Jesus came to destroy the works of Satan (**1 John 3:8**) to restore man to his dignity, glory, and purpose. Even though the kingdom of God has been won for us by Jesus, Satan, the evil one, is still fighting hard to deny man of it.

Hence, the gospel in Mathew 11:12 states:

"Right from the birth of John the Baptist,
the Kingdom of God suffereth violence, but the radicals taketh it by force."

-Mathew 11:12

So it is in paradise that the soul and spirit that are upright are kept after judgment until the end of days, which no man knows but God; Jesus will come to his own, and they will reappear, resurrect to meet Jesus from Heaven (paradise), whence they shall be caught up with him in glory.

"For the Lord, Himself shall descend from Heaven with a shout, with the voice of
an archangel and with the trumpet of God; and the dead in Christ shall rise first.
Then we that are alive and remain shall be caught up together with them in the
clouds, to meet the Lord in the air, so shall we ever be with the Lord."

I Thessalonians 4:16-17

Paradise, in essence, is not heaven itself. Instead is the third heaven, a place of supernatural supreme bliss, where the souls & spirits of those departed from their mortal bodies and are upright in Christ Jesus, their souls are kept to be rested after judgment. It is where the Kingdom of God operates, as it is in heaven; recall our Lord's Prayer.

I knew a man in Christ above fourteen years ago (whether in the body, I cannot tell, or whether
out of the body, I cannot tell, God knoweth) such as one caught up to the third heaven.
"And I knew such a man (whether in the body or out of the body,
I cannot tell, God knoweth) How He was caught up in paradise
and heard unspeakable words, which it is not lawful for a man to utter."

II Corinthians 12:2-4

Once a man dies, the body, which is dust, returns to dust, the soul is judged, and the spirit is sentenced and sentenced to paradise (third heaven) till the end of days or to hell. Judgment is not delayed because your soul will judge you instantly (**Luke 16:19-31**). No eye has seen God, except He that descended from above. . . Jesus Christ has ascended. So, when our days on earth are finished, our earthly vessel (body) will dissolve away, and the soul and spirit will transcend for judgment and reward, respectively.

"1. For we know that if our Earthly house of this tabernacle were dissolved, we have a building of God, a house not made with hands, eternal in the heavens (paradise)".

4. For we that are in this tabernacle do groan, being burdened not for that we Would be unclothed; but clothed upon, <u>that mortality might be swallowed up to life.</u>

5. Now he that brought us for the selfsame thing is God, who also hath given unto us the earnest of the spirit.

6. Therefore, we are always confident, <u>knowing that whilst we are at home in the Body, we are absent from the Lord.</u>

7. (For we walk by faith, not by sight)

8. <u>We are confident, I say, and willing somewhat to be absent from the body and present with the Lord.</u>

9. Therefore, we labour that, whether present or absent, we may be accepted of him.

10<u>. For we must all appear before the judgment seat of Christ, that everyone may receive the things done in his body, according to what he hath done, whether good or bad.</u>

II Corinthians 5:1, 4-10

When the end of the days finally arrives, all the saints whose souls have been judged and found not guilty, residing in paradise, the third heaven will re-appear (resurrect) again, coming down with Jesus Divine in the cloud. Men who are still living will be caught up (raptured) to meet them in the cloud with great triumph, leaving their mortal bodies behind. These men have paid the prize; they believed in Jesus as their Lord and personal saviour and had walked in his statues. They will finally be compensated for they have fought and defeated Satan, by the word of their testimony (i.e., their belief) and by the blood of the lamb JESUS.

"And one of the elders answered, saying unto me
'What are these which are arrayed in white robes? And whence came they.'
And I said unto him. Sir, thou knowest. And he said to me,
These came out of great tribulation and have washed
their robes and made them white in the blood of the lamb.
Therefore, are they before the throne of God and serve him day and night
in his temple, and he that sitteth on the throne shall dwell among them…
they shall hunger no more, neither thirst any more, neither shall the sunlight on them
nor any heat. For the lamb amid the throne shall feed them
and lead them unto living fountains of water,
and God shall wipe away all tears from their eyes."

-Revelation 7:13-17

A new paradise, which is heaven, is being revealed. The former is hidden. Hence, the Kingdom of God is not only established but made manifest, enjoyment forever, with no more tears, pain, death, thirst, hatred, or wickedness…

Brethren,

13. If there is no resurrection (reappearance) of the dead, then is Christ not risen?

17. If Christ is not raised, your faith is vain; you are yet in your sins.

18. Then they also which are fallen asleep in Christ are perishable finally.

19. IF IN THIS LIFE ONLY, WE HAVE HOPE OF CHRIST, WE ARE OF ALL MEN ARE MOST MISERABLE.

11 cor. 5; 13-19

Life continues…

The question still lingers: Is man an eternal spirit?

Let us try again and visualize how JESUS also sees 'man'. JESUS, who is not carnally minded, should be our central insight.

A man named Nicodemus, one of the elites of the Pharisees, on a perfect night, sneaked out of his compound and went to JESUS. He religiously asked him an excellent question; perhaps he was convinced that JESUS came from GOD, and he wanted to know more about this teaching called "SALVATION" from JESUS.

And Jesus said to him.

"Except a man is born – again, he cannot see the kingdom of God."

-John 3:3

And this man Nicodemus, though an elite, could not comprehend what JESUS meant. No wonder the bible says that a carnally minded man could not understand the things of the spirit; it would be like foolishness unto him* **I Cor.; 2:14**

Unrelenting, Nicodemus asked JESUS one more question.

"How can a man be born when he is old? Can he enter his mother's womb the second time and be born?"

- John 3:4

And Jesus kindly answered him.

"Verily, verily I said unto you, except a man be born of water and the spirit, he cannot enter into the kingdom of God".

- John 3:5

In verse 6, Jesus emphasizes.,

"That which is born of the flesh is flesh. That which is born of the spirit is spirit."

- John 3:5, 6

Man is spirit, born of the spirit, and GOD is spirit. And the spirit could only be born again by the renewal of the soul, which could be activated by living in the subjective consciousness of the mastermind. I will explain these further in the next chapter.

Water could only cleanse the body (accepted) by means of baptism, which had a spiritual undertone, but that is the outward man. The spirit-man (spiritual nature of man), the inward man, which is the real man, was born-again and renewed.

People used to say *Baptism* and could not perceive that there are two types of baptism, but Jesus knows (**John 3**):

a. One of the waters that represents or symbolizes one of the spirits; it cleans the outward man and marks or symbolizes what is to come.
b. The baptism of the spirit is the baptism of the inner man, which renews the soul and is activated by the word of God.

Jesus bears witness to this when he prays for the sanctification of his disciples.

"Sanctify them through thy truth; thy word is truth."

-John 17:17

The spirit man is what is renewed and makes a new creature in Christ Jesus; it is not the physical body. The spirit is being renewed daily; it does not die; it is Jesus's opinion and his teaching for us to know that we are not merely physical bodies.

"But though our outward man perishes,
yet the inward man is renewed day by day."

-2 Corinthians 4:16

Were you born – again? What does this mean?

When the mind is full of darkness, it destroys the nature of GOD in us; however, the renewal of one's mind makes one in line with God's Divine nature. Being born-again, this renewal of the mind is nothing but believing in Christ Jesus and observing (imitating) his statue.

"And this is life eternal; that they might know thee,
the only true God and Jesus Christ, whom thou have sent."

-John 17:3

"Therefore, if any man (spirit-man) be in Christ, he is a new creature (renewal),
old things are passed away, behold ALL THINGS have become new."

2 Corinthians 5:17

What are 'ALL THINGS'?

Listen carefully:

A black man could not be turned into a white man if he got born-again; a man with bald hair will still be bald, even after being born-again (i.e., being renewed).

So, being born again and all things becoming new in this, the spirit (inward man) is being transformed, and the nature of God is activated. Man is a spirit and needs to be spiritually conscious.

The spirit, being transformed, is by the renewal of the soul (mind), and this is positive and real by the word of God because **the word of God is quick and sharper than a two-edged sword, piercing even to the dividing asunder of SOUL and SPIRIT and the joints and marrows (BODY) and is a discerner of the thought and intents of the heart (MIND). – Hebrews 4:12**

God is a spiritual entity. Man acquires his being from God and, by so doing, shares in the being of God. In this way, man is said to be a spirit, especially if man develops himself spiritually. As man renews himself in the Lord, he keeps getting better spiritually. For this, we say that the spirit could only be born again by the renewal of the soul, which is activated by living in total consciousness of the essentials knowable to a mastermind. The spirit man is the real man. He is the one who is born-again and renewed. Such a person works for Jesus since he or she knows him and aims to enjoy heaven with him.

[2] And do not be conformed to this world, <u>but be transformed by the renewing of your mind, that you may prove what is that good and acceptable and perfect will of God.</u> -Romans 12:2 NKJV Bible.

> **"To be carnally minded is death, but to be spiritually minded is life & peace."**
>
> **- Romans 8:6**

Finally, my people recalling the topic of this chapter:

> **"These things have I written unto you that believe on the name of the Son of God; that you may know that ye have ETERNAL SPIRIT."**
>
> **- I John 5:13**

Chapter THREE

THE MIND OF MAN (SOUL)

The mind is the soul of man because the mind controls the whole being of man, in that, the state of mind justifies or condemns the soul, as the soul is to the spirit (in Pari-per sue)

The mind (soul) is the willpower of man given to him freely by GOD –the nature of GOD.

The mind regulates the dignity of the human person; it controls all the activities of human existence and needs to be tamed.

Being willpower, when under control, results in good things, while, when abused, corrupts the whole man.

The mind and the soul influence man's thoughts, sense of reasoning, activities and actions, and emotions.

Man being a spirit, got born-again by the renewal of the soul.

"Create in me a clean heart (soul/mind), O GOD, and renew a right spirit within me.

– Psalm 51:10

It is only the mind of God that can renew a right spirit within man. Once the mind is corrupt, the inner man will be filled with filthy spirits and evil conscience.

Baptism sincerely employs the cleansing of the flesh and the rebirth of the spirit; the soul of man does not get born-again; it is only the spirit. But for this to happen, the soul/mind of man needs to be renewed by the word of God. The soul is very inflammable by what it sees and hears, so the spirit-conscious man lives by faith and not by sight. And the soul needs to be dealt with. Man's mind (soul) is very flexible and could be twisted. Only the word of GOD can be a guide and light unto it. It could be derailed by naughtiness, filthiness, and attachment to mundane things if left alone.

No wonder St. James was warning his fellow believers about the deeds of the soul, and he admonishes:

"Of his own will begat He us with the word of truth; that we should be a kind of first fruits of His creatures. Wherefore, my beloved brethren, let every man be swift to hear, slow to speak, slow to wrath of which worketh not the righteousness of GOD. Wherefore lay apart all filthiness and superfluity of naughtiness, and <u>receive with meekness the engrafted word, which can save your souls</u>.

-James 1: 18-21(KJV)

From the above text, there is no argument that Brother James was talking to his fellow believers. Though they were born-again by their spirit man, their souls and the intents of their minds are not all right and need to be guided.

Though man is spirit, the inward man, the real man receives eternal life and is born-again, yet his intellect, which composes his soul, must be continually dealt with. And the weapon of this is the word of GOD, which is the will of GOD.

> **"For the word of GOD is quick, and powerful, and sharper than any two-edged sword, piercing even to dividing asunder of soul and spirit and of the joints and marrow (body) and is a discerner of the thoughts (mind), and intents of the heart (soul)."**
>
> **-Hebrews 4:12**

THE GREATEST WARFARE

The thoughts of man (intellect) and the intents of the heart are being controlled by the mind of man, which is the soul. It is the greatest war; man must fight to progress in the stability of his or her being. The imagination of the heart and the mind's negative thoughts are all strongholds and must be dealt with.

> **"For though we walk in the flesh, we do not war after the flesh. For the weapon of our warfare are not carnal, but mighty through God to pull down strongholds. Casting down imaginations, and every high thing that exalted itself against the knowledge of GOD, and bringing into captivity, every thought to the obedience of Christ."**
>
> **II Corinthians 10:3-5**

Our greatest warfare is not with the flesh; it must be with our mind, every imagination that exalted itself against the knowledge, the word, and the will of GOD. Because **as a man thinketh, so is he (Prov. 23:7)** St. Paul also teaches about the mind of man, and he says to the saints in ROME:

> **"And be not conformed to this world: but be Ye transformed by the renewing of your mind, that Ye may prove what is that good, and acceptable and perfect will of God."**
>
> **Romans 12: 2**

Man, as a spirit, living in a physical body and having a living soul, needs his soul to be saved or restored by renewing his mind with the word of GOD. It is the word that renews our minds, renews our souls, and saves our souls. When our minds get renewed with the word of God, then we cooperate with the word of GOD by thinking in line with the word of GOD. Hence, we can know and prove the permissive and perfect will of God. Brethren, it is time to get your mind renewed.

> **"Let this mind be in you, which was also in Christ Jesus."**
>
> **-Philippians 2:5**

The weapon to win this fight of the mind is the positivity of our thoughts.

"Finally, Brethren: whatsoever things are <u>True,</u>
Whatsoever things are <u>Honest,</u>
Whatsoever things are <u>Just,</u>
Whatsoever things are <u>Pure,</u>
Whatsoever things are <u>Lovely,</u>
Whatsoever things are of a <u>Good Report,</u>
If there be any virtue, and if there be any <u>Praise</u>
<u>'THINK'</u> about these things."

-Philippians 4:8

Chapter FOUR

THE POWER OF THE MIND (SOUL)

"For as a man thinketh in his heart (mind), so is he."

-Proverbs 23:7

The mind of man, the 'mastermind', is dynamic and flexible; it is a powerful tool in a man's life, which can build a man or destroy him. Metaphorically, the mastermind is the sailor or captain of this boat called Man. The willpower of man, which controls all the affairs of man, is centralized in the mind.

There are two types of minds, but before I proceed to emphasize them and how powerful they are in controlling the affairs of man, I would like to redirect our thoughts to things happening around our world.

Let us figure out our facts from this man people called **'madman'**. What makes him a madman? Why is he mad? Considering that his body looks nice and healthy, his eyes, nose, ears, legs, etc., everything is in order. Biologically, all the hormones in his/her body are perfect; even his brain is normal. But one thing is clear. HE IS A MADMAN. A layman will say… 'the brain is not all right'. However, the mind controls the brain.

There is nothing wrong with the head; the problem is this: as a man thinketh in his mind, so is he (**Proverbs 23:7**). The problem is with the MIND.

Consider this one, which is an existing phenomenon also in a governmental Parastatal, whereby the heads of such a government are virtually corrupt in their mind; nevertheless, there are minorities whose minds are correct, but the whole system will be corrupt, there will be a lot of merchants of mismanagement in such a governmental body. (As a man thinketh, so is he – THE MIND).

Dealing with spiritual matters has made me understand that there is an occult practice or manipulation called the OCCULTIC MANIPULATION OF THE MASTERMIND.

And at this periphery, I would like to let you know that, before anything happens physically, it has already happened in the spiritual realm. If you know how to close your eyes, you will see what open eyes cannot see. He, who has ears, let him hear and understand. If one can control their spiritual realm, one will have peace and rest always.

Please, my dear son/daughter of man, have you asked yourself a question of this nature:
→ Why do people commit suicide?
→ Why do they burn themselves up?
→ Why does a man shoot his wife, child(ren) and himself on a perfect day?
→ Why could someone stab their parent/girlfriend, poison her husband, etc.?
→ Why do people pour acid on their fellows?
→ Why do others do good things and others do bad things?
→ Why do people rape? ...etc. A question one may ask.

In the spiritual world, say ASTRAL OR MARINE KINGDOM OR EVEN TERRESTRIAL KINGDOM, somebody who is living in the objective mind of carnality could be manipulated by controlling his mastermind spiritually. Before he could know it, he would see himself doing what he could never imagine in life to do, such as killing their mother or even their child; you can see them happening in our world today; you can read them in the daily newspapers.

Hence, I would like us to know that two types of mind exist in the life of man
a) The subjective mind (sane mind)
b) The objective mind (corrupt mind)

SUBJECTIVE MIND
People living under the consciousness of a subjective mind have full control of their minds because they are being led by the spirit of God, who lives in them and revitalizing their mortal bodies. Their souls are being subjected in line and tune with the nature and consciousness of God. Such people's minds could not think of evil things; their consciences had been purified, and their minds were renewed and justified by the word of God.
The word of God has renewed such people's minds. The word of God has transformed their thoughts, and they cannot do anything wrong because their conscience speaks. Their thoughts are pure, and they cannot be manipulated via occult means.

OBJECTIVE MIND:
About 90% of the world population today lives under the consciousness of the objective mind, which is why many bad things are happening. They have their conscience being seared with a hot iron, and they are no longer in control of their mind. Their minds become evil and corrupt. When their mind objectively suggests

to them to smoke, they do, drink poison, they do; commit suicide, they do; they do fornicate, they do rape, kill, murder, steal, etc.; they do all these things without recognition. They are easily manipulated via occult means. People living under the consciousness of the objective mind are carnally minded and live in the flesh, and they do not have peace.

"To be carnally minded is death, but to be spiritually minded is life and peace."

-Romans 8:6

And the image of God is not in them because as they do all these things, they extinguish the spirit of God in them, which can revitalize their mortal body and soul, a living soul.

"<u>Because that, when they knew God, they glorified him not as God, neither were thankful;</u>
<u>but became vain in their imaginations, and their foolish hearts (mind) was darkened.</u>
<u>Professing themselves to be wise, they become fools.</u> And changed the glory of the incorruptible God,
into an image made like to corruptible man, and to birds, and four-footed beasts and creeping things.
Therefore, God also gave them up to uncleanness through the <u>lusts of their own</u>
<u>hearts</u>(minds) to dishonour their own bodies between themselves.
Who changed the truth of God into a lie and worshipped and served the
creature more than the creator, who is blessed forever, Amen!
For this cause, God gave them up unto vile affection, for even their woman did
change the natural use into that which is against nature (lesbianism)
And likewise, also the men, leaving the natural use of the woman, burned in
their lust one toward another, men with men working unseemly (homosexuality)
receiving in themselves that which recompense of their error which was meet.
And even as they did not like to retain God in their knowledge, God gave them over
to a reprobate (objective) mind to do those things which are not convenient.
Being filled with all unrighteousness, fornication, wickedness, maliciousness, full of
envy, murder, debate, deceit, malignity, whispers. Backbiters, haters of God, despiteful,
proud boasters, inventors of evil things, disobedient to parents, without understanding,
covenant breakers, without natural affection, implacable, unmerciful:
Who knowing the judgment of God, that they which commit such things are worthy
of death, not only do the same but have pleasure in them that do them."

-Romans 1:21-32

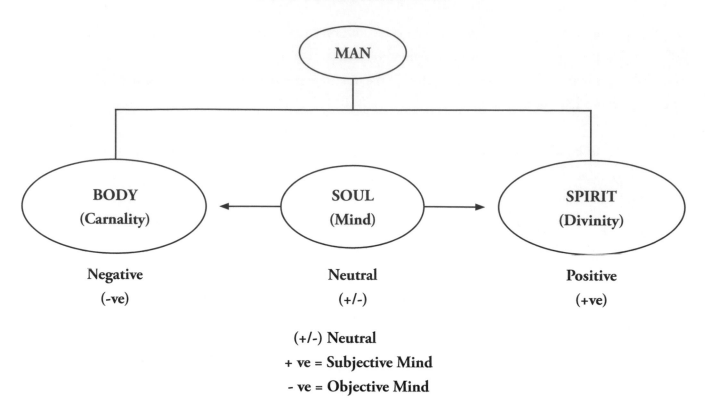

(+/-) Neutral
+ ve = Subjective Mind
- ve = Objective Mind

When the mind of man is subjected to the subjective consciousness of the mastermind, it profits from the spiritual nature of man, which is the real man. Still, when the mind of man is subjected to the objective consciousness of the mind, it profits from the carnal nature of man, which makes man decline from the image, likeness, consciousness and nature of GOD, and man starts living carnally and becomes full of evil.

The mind of man is neutral and flexible, depicting the willpower of man given to him by GOD as a gift to humanity. The power to make choices. The mind could be positive or negative. So, for the mind to be positive, it needs to be renewed by the word of GOD, which can restore the soul to nature, will, the consciousness of GOD and then, will be able to save the SOUL of man. This is the POWER OF THE MIND.

Considering Biblical teachings of the mind, I would like to figure out how our Lord JESUS, the author and finisher of our faith, considers the mind so powerful in the affairs of a man's life.
Please come with me to the GOSPEL of **Mathews 15:17-20**

> "**Do you not yet understand that whatsoever that entered in at the**
> **mouth goeth into the belly and is cast out into the draught?**
> **But those things that proceed out of the mouth come forth from the heart (mind) and defile man.**
> **From the heart (mind), proceed evil thoughts, murders, adulteries,**
> **fornications, thefts, false witness, and blasphemies.**
> **These are the things that defile a man.**"

-Matthew 15:17-20

Here, JESUS enumerates to his disciples the power of the mind. He is trying to let them know that the thoughts of his mind are controlling the affairs in the life of a man. Basically, in this text, JESUS is emphasizing the **objective mind of man.**

From verse 18 of the above-mentioned text, you can agree with me about the robust nature of the mind because every thought of the mind is what proceeds out of the mouth of man. Recalling this bible portion, which says that **the power of life and death is in the tongue (Proverbs 18:21)**, you can also agree with me that, **out of the abundance of the heart (mind), the mouth (tongue) speaks, therefore**, the power of life and death, is in the MIND, the power of the mind.

Considering the next biblical text, it still explains the power of the mind. The mind regulates the positive or negative confession of man and influences his life.

> **"For with the heart (mind), man believes unto righteousness,**
> **and with the mouth (tongue) confession is made unto salvation."**
>
> **Romans 10:10**

Considering another word of JESUS.

> **"Ye have heard that it was said by them of old time; thou shalt not commit**
> **adultery; but I say unto you, that whosoever looked on a woman to lust after**
> **her hath committed adultery with her already <u>in his heart</u> (mind)."**
>
> **Matthew 5: 27-28**

Once again, you can depict the power of the mind in action from what JESUS is teaching us. As a man thinks in his mind (heart), so is he. (Know that people misinterpret the mind with the heart out of carnality and ignorance; I do make it for you to understand that the heart is an organ in the body's circulatory system that pumps blood.) Please take note that the heart in the Bible depicts the mind (soul).

Another example of the power of the mind could be delineated from the actions of Lucifer, the leviathan from the scripture.

> ❖ **How art thou fallen from heaven, O Lucifer, son of the morning! How art thou cut down to**
> **the ground, which didst weaken the nations! <u>For thou hast said in thine heart (mind)</u>. I will**
> **ascend into heaven, I will exalt my throne above the stars of God: I will sit also upon the mount**
> **of the congregation, in the sides of the north: I will ascend above the heights of the clouds; I**
> **will be like the most High. Yet thou shalt be brought down to hell, to the sides of the pit.**
>
> **-Isaiah 14:12-15**

❖ Son of man, take up lamentation upon the king of Tyrus, and say unto him, thus saith the Lord God, thou sealest up the sun, full of wisdom, and perfect in beauty. Thou hast been in Eden, the garden of GOD, every precious stone was thy covering, the sardius, topaz, and the diamond, the beryl, the onyx and the jasper, the sapphire, the emerald, and the carbuncle and gold: the workmanship of thy tabrets on thy pipes was prepared in thee in the day that thou was created.

❖ Thou art the anointed cherub that covereth; and I have set thee so: thou was upon the holy mountain of God, thou walked up and down in the midst of the stones of fire. Thou wast perfect in thy ways from the day that thou were created, till iniquity was found in thee. By the multitude of thy merchandise, they have filled the midst of thee with violence, and thou hast sinned: therefore I will cast as profane thee out of the mountain of God: and I will destroy thee, O covering cherub, from the midst of stones of fire. <u>Thine heart</u> was lifted because of thy beauty, thou have <u>corrupted</u> thy wisdom by reason of thy brightness: I will cast thee to the ground, I will lay thee before kings, that they may behold thee.

-Ezekiel 28:12-17 KJV

The above biblical texts show that LUCIFER, the anointed cherub that covereth, was perfect in all his ways until iniquity was found in him. What was wrong? – **His mind**.

His mind became corrupt; the way he thinks becomes very objective in the parlance of consciousness. The mind of man condemns and sets free. Is your mind in the negative, or is it in the positive right now? There is no judgment on the last day; only the MASTERMIND of man will judge man. The mind is potential.

Know clearly, son of man, that the power of life and death is the mind; it can condemn a man (Mathew 5:28) and free a man. Therefore, knowing the power of the mind, Man ought to decline himself unto the subjective consciousness of the mind and not the objective; by then, can MAN operate under the perfect will and not under the permissive will? Everything of faith, sin, pride, and humility comes from the mind, THE POWER OF THE MIND.

Chapter FIVE

SPIRIT CONSCIOUS

For a man to perfect himself in the subjective consciousness of the mastermind, he must be spirit-conscious, sensitive, and active.

Man being spirit conscious is to know who he is and try to reign in the spiritual realm. This is the dignity of man.

Science has enveloped man, and scientific processes are the order of the day; Man is living in the mental realm. Even some so-called men of God preach the WORD with the enticing word of mouth, man's wisdom, that is mentally enriched since they (Pastors and preachers) can read and understand. They are not spiritual. Most gospel singers are no longer spirit-conscious; they are being overwhelmed by religious spirit and sing because they have refined voices.

> **"For Christ sent me not to baptize, but to preach the gospel:**
> **Not with wisdom of words, lest the words of Christ should be made of none effect.**
> **For the preaching of the cross is to them that perish foolishness <u>but unto us</u>**
> **<u>which are saved, it is the Power of God.</u> For it is written, I will destroy the wisdom**
> **of the wise and bring to nothing the understanding of the prudent".**
> **-I Corinthians 1:17-19**

> **"And my speech and my preaching were not with enticing words of man's**
> **wisdom, <u>but in demonstrating of the spirit and power:</u> That your faith**
> **<u>should not stand in the wisdom of men but in the power of God</u>".**
> **-I Corinthians 2:4-5**

> **"For the kingdom of God is not in word but in power."**
> **- I Corinthians 4:20**

Carnality has been the coat of arms for man, who is meant to be spiritual; because He is a spirit being, He is not what he seems outside; he is an inward man.

Until man begins to realize who he is and will always be and starts living in the supernatural, being spiritually conscious, that will enable HIM to visualize & subject his mind to the subjective consciousness and reality of the mastermind, man will continue to miss out; and our world will become more deteriorated, because of objective mindedness.

Hence, the duty of man and the dignity of man is to begin to realize and confess that He is A SPIRIT BEING, HE HAS A SOUL, AND HE LIVES IN A BODY. This is not fiction. It is REAL.

Chapter SIX

MEDITATION – BRINGING THE MIND HOME

"Let the words of my mouth and the meditation of my heart (mind - soul) be acceptable in thy sight. O' Lord, my strength, my redeemer."

-Psalm 19:14

The dictionary defines meditation as . . . a plan mentally designed, an exercise of the mind in especially religious contemplation on/upon a subject.

In my understanding of meditation, it is that specific period of quiet time that our minds find that natural peace, which renews our spiritual strength and the Holy Ghost guiding us, speaking to us in His quiet voice to give us directions.

Meditation is the road to enlightenment. Meditation is the greatest gift one can give himself in this life. Through meditation, the Holy Spirit guides us as we obey the Holy Spirit; He speaks, comforts, teaches, and reveals mysteries to us.

Through meditation, we undertake the journey to discover our true nature, hence finding the stability and confidence of our existence. In meditation, you hear with your spiritual ear, you see with your spiritual eyes, and understanding exceeds that of the natural sense of perception. In meditation, the mind is home.

The Bible shows how JESUS used to go to a solitary place where he constantly meditates in prayer alone. Why does he choose a quiet place? Meditation could also be termed QUIET TIME. See . . . {**Mark 1:35, Luke 4:42, Luke 5:16, Luke 6:12 etc.**}.

In our daily lives, we often find ourselves distracted by various concerns for almost 22 hours a day. These distractions prevent us from being in touch with our true selves, and instead, we engage in never-ending activities, objective thinking, and anxious struggles. We live our lives amidst the chaos of haste and aggression, competing, grasping, and possessing, forever burdening ourselves with unnecessary activities and preoccupations.

There is no favourable time to pray, read the Bible, have quiet time, object the mastermind to natural peace, and wait upon the Lord to review our authentic self, the spirit man, with quiet time, payer, and fasting.

"They that wait upon the Lord; the Lord will renew their strength,
They will mount on wings like eagles; they shall run and not be weary,
They shall walk and shall not faint."

-Isaiah 40; 31

TO MEDITATE

- Is to make a complete break with how we "normally" operate, for it is a state of mind free of all cares and concerns, in which there is no competition, no desire to possess or grasp at anything, no intense and anxious struggle and no hunger to achieve; an ambition- less state where there is neither acceptance nor rejection, neither hope no fear, a state in which we slowly begin to realize all those emotions and concepts that have imprisoned us into the space of natural simplicity.

Through meditation, we train our minds,
Knowing fully how flexible and feasible the mind is, anything is possible if we train the mastermind.
In this wicked world of the evil generation, our mind has already been trained to such an extent that we are perfectly trained to be jealous, grasp, trained to react angrily to whatever provokes us. We are trained to such an extent that these negative emotions rise spontaneously without even trying to generate them. So, everything is a question of training and the power to Habit.

Devote the mind to confusion, and we know too well, if we are honest, that it will become a dark master of confusion. Train a man's mind to terrorism; in a lifetime, he is a terrorist. Devote the mind to meditation, to the task of freeing itself from illusion, and you will find out that, with time, patience, discipline and the proper training, our mind will begin to unknot itself, and essential bliss and clarity will materialize.

Meditation aims to awaken the sky-like nature of the mind and introduce us to what we are: our unchanging pure awareness, which underlines the whole of our existence. In the stillness and silence of meditation, we glimpse and return to that profound inner nature that we have so long-ago lost sight of amid the busyness and distractions of our minds.

We are fragmented into so many different aspects, to the extent that the centre (the mind) cannot hold anymore and our life and being keep falling apart. We do not know who we are or what aspects of ourselves we should identify with or believe in. So many contradictory voices (dictate and feelings fight for control over our inner lives that we find ourselves scattered everywhere, in all directions, leaving nobody at home. MEDITATION, then, is bringing the mind home.

SOME TIPS ABOUT MEDITATION

Remember: a method is only a means, not the meditation itself. By practicing this method skillfully, you reach the perfection of that pure state of real presence, the actual meditation, where there is peace of mind. Meditation is just getting used to the practice of meditation. Meditation is not striving but naturally becoming assimilated into it.

As you continue to practice the method, then meditation slowly arises. You cannot do meditation; it must happen spontaneously when we have perfected the practice. Even if you fail at first, keep on; you will succeed and merit joy from it.

However, for meditation to happen, calm and auspicious conditions must be created. Before we have mastery over our mind, we need to calm its environment first. Now, the mind is like a candle flame: unstable, flickering, constantly changing, fanned by the violent winds of our thoughts and emotions. On the other hand, once we have formed stability in our meditation, noises and disturbances of every kind will have far less impact. As you meditate, you will find the answers to most life problems.

IN SUMMARY

Meditation is only occult if one makes it to be. In meditation, you must be calm, abiding, have peace of mind, pray to God, and wait upon him. fasting and prayer help make this practice easier and beneficial.

Chapter SEVEN

THE LINK BETWEEN BODY, SOUL (MIND) AND SPIRIT

"Create in me a <u>clean heart (mind),</u> O God, and <u>renew</u> a right <u>spirit within me</u>".
Cast me not away from thy presence; and take not away from me
thy presence, and take not <u>thy Holy Spirit</u> from me

- Psalm 51:10-11

The mind (soul) links the body and the spirit. Though it constantly fights to make them live in harmony, the body (flesh) and the spirit are antagonistic. This is excellent warfare. And in this warfare, it is expected of the spirit to win and be the captain of the soul. However, for the spirit to be the victor, the mind, which is the soul, must be clean and spotless. Invariably, if the mind is filthy, it favours the flesh; this is the golden rule. Let's put it this way before I proceed further trying to link the body, soul, and spirit.

- With the spirit, I contact the spiritual realm.
- With the body, I contact the physical realm and
- With the soul (mind), I contact the intellectual realm; put, one can reason and think.
- Feeling is the voice of the body.
- Conscience is the voice of the Spirit.
- Reason is the voice of the mind (soul)

The body and the spirit are antagonistic; the mind is the judge. The word of God renews and sanctifies our mind, which can save our soul (mind).

"Sanctify them through thy truth; thy word is truth."

-John 17:17

Continuation and meditation in the word of God make us act in line with the nature of God because the word of God is the will of God. Then, can we live as we are meant to live? In as much as we live in the consciousness of God by meditating on his word, we grow spiritually, living the life of God, Eternal life. However, in all these, we should not be ignorant of the devices of the enemy, the devil, trying to entrap us with the lust of the flesh (body), the outward man.

"I beseech you therefore, brethren, by the mercies of God, that <u>ye present your bodies a living sacrifice, holy, acceptable unto God</u>, which is your reasonable service."

-Romans 12:1

"And be not conformed to this world but be ye transformed <u>by the renewing of your mind, that ye may prove what that good and acceptable perfect will of God is.</u>"

-Romans 12:2

Firstly, we cannot live a good and acceptable life, and we cannot do the will of God if we live in the flesh. That is why St. Paul while admonishing his fellow brethren, pleaded that they might submit their bodies under subjection, which is their greatest sacrifice.

He continued to tell them not to conform to the things of this world, the lust of the flesh, the lust of the eye and the pride of life, etc.; though living in the world, they should transform their livelihood by renewing their mind. However, the mind can only be renewed by <u>doing</u> the word. Renewal of the mind saves the soul, while the lust of flesh condemns the soul. And when the soul is condemned, we lose contact with the nature, life and will of God; and the spirit of God which dwells in us decamps, and man being a spirit has no more guidance, the light departs, and darkness envelopes man and the mind of man becomes objective. When the body is subjected to the will of God, by obeying the word of GOD, the spiritual nature of man, the inward man, the real man, wins.

"Thy word is the lamp unto my feet and a light unto my path."

-Psalm 119:105

Let us see how this body (flesh) affects some men of God who subject themselves to God's will. Firstly, in the New Testament, St. Paul, a spiritual giant, a great apostle, and a holy man of God; could not even deny the agony of the flesh he was passing through- though spiritually sensitive, to dominate the inward man, and Paul says:

"But I keep my body and bring it into subjection, lest that by any means when I have preached to others, I should be a castaway (disapproved)."

- I Corinthians 9:27

Here, Brother Paul is testifying about what he does to his body. He "Paul," the honest Paul, says, "I keep my body and bring it under SUBJECTION". This is the real Paul, the inward man, who has become a new creature filled with the Holy Spirit. Instead of letting the body dominate the inward man, he ensures the reverse is the case, and the word of God is the weapon of this great warfare, even though we exist in the flesh (body). We do not do this warfare carnally; it is the word of God that triumphs over us* Listen carefully; it is our spirit and our flesh that is in warfare, and the battle takes place in the mind; our duty is to equip the spirit with the sword of the spirit which is not carnal and is the weapon of the spirit, and is the word of God divine. The winner of this fight is determined by how we channel our minds (thoughts, reasoning, emotions, sensitivities, etc.).

"For though we walk in the flesh, we do not war after the flesh.
For the weapons of warfare are not carnal, but mighty through God to the pulling down of strongholds, casting down imaginations and every high thing that exalted itself against the knowledge of God and bringing into captivity every _thought_ to the obedience of Christ."

-II Corinthians 10:3-5

Listen,

The spirit man does not need to war against the flesh but rather to renew the mind; then, the flesh will be subjected.

Considering the faith of our father, the patriarch (**David**); one could ask a question.

David, a man after God's own heart, in some cases, sees himself doing the things he does not imagine doing, seemingly, his flesh controlling him, such as in sleeping with Beersheba, Uriah's wife: In all this warfare, which he could not imagine; he exclaimed!

"Wherewithal shall a young man cleanse his way? By taking heed to it according to thy word."

-Psalm 119:9

I love David so much; even as he asked the question, He answered it. He is indeed a man after God's heart.

Considering **Job**, a perfect man, could you imagine?

He knows that the lust of the flesh, the lust of the eye, etc., is a powerful trouble to a spiritual man; he likewise did like St. Paul and gave himself conditions by making a covenant.

"I make a covenant with mine eyes; why should I think upon a maid."

-Job 31:1

In other words, Job asks why he must lust after a girl.

Chapter EIGHT

CONSCIENCE - LIVING IN THE SUBJECTIVE CONSCIOUSNESS OF THE MASTER MIND

"And Paul earnestly beholding the council said, Men and Brethren, I have lived in all good conscience before God until today."

-Acts 23:1

Conscience is the voice of the human spirit – spirit man, which is active (neither deaf nor dumb) when an individual subjects him or herself to the level of living in the subjective consciousness of the mastermind (soul).

A person who has not been born again could not follow the voice of his spirit. His spirit is unregenerated. His conscience would permit him to do just anything.

However, when one has the life and nature of God in him, his conscience will not permit them to do just anything. And if one is born-again, having his mind renewed, not conforming to the things of this world, such a one has the Life of God.

Listen carefully; the mind frees or condemns us, which means our conscience tells our spirit man whether we are free.

"For if our heart (mind) condemns us, God is greater than our heart (mind), and knoweth all things. Beloved, if our heart (mind) condemns us not, then have we have confidence toward God."

-I John 3:20-21

The heart (mind) judges; it frees or condemns, but once we start to get our mind renewed via the word of God, God is more significant than our mind and must forgive us. He is greater than the mind. He forgives and overlooks our ignorance. Once we are forgiven by God and our mind does not condemn us henceforth, our conscience whispers to our spirit, and our spirit bears witness that we are God's children and God's life, and nature are in us. On the contrary, some people's minds are corrupt and have been seared with a hot iron.

Listening, they cannot hear; looking, they cannot see; the God of this world has blinded their mind; hence, living under an objective and reprobate mind, do ungodly things. (**II Corinthians 4:3-4**).

"Speaking lies in hypocrisy; having their conscience seared with a hot iron."

-I Timothy 4:2

"Because that, when they knew God; they glorified him not as God; neither were thankful; but become vain in their imaginations (reasoning's) and their foolish heart (mind) was darkened."

-Romans 1:21-22

Professing themselves to be wise, they become fools.

And while they did not like to retain God in their knowledge, God gave them over to a <u>reprobate mind</u> to do those things which are convenient, being filled with all unrighteousness, fornication, wickedness, covetousness, maliciousness, full of envy, murder, debate, deceit, malignity, whispers backbites, hater of God, despiteful, proud, boasters, inventors of evil things, disobedient to parents; without understanding convent breakers, without natural affection: implacable, unmerciful.

-Romans 1:28-31

In his book on the justification of faith, John Henry Newman states that conscience is a moral sense of duty. Conscience is considered a moral sense, in an intellectual sentiment, but it is always emotional. Therefore, it involves the recognition of living objects. Inanimate things cannot stir our affections; these are correlative with persons.

When we feel the same sorrowful and broken-hearted emotion on doing wrong, which overwhelms us on hurting a mother, and when we experience the same serene and satisfying delight in doing right that we feel on receiving praise from a father, we have within us an image of some person whom we love and respect. Their smile brings us happiness, we yearn for their presence, we direct our pleas towards them, and their anger troubles us and makes us feel miserable. These feelings in us are such as requiring for their exciting cause an intelligent being . . .

CONSCIENCE IS THE VOICE OF THE HUMAN SPIRIT.

Chapter NINE

FAITH (THE CONDITION OF THE MIND)

Faith, which is a state of mind, contributes enormously to the nature of man and, thus, needs to be applied to / and checked in our livelihood.

Fear is also a state of the mind and is the opposite of faith. Why is God pleased with any act of faith? He dislikes fear, which is why fear is one of the tools of Satan to hoodwink man.

All the teachings of Jesus Christ and most of his practices, which we call miracles today, are all exhibitions of faith he teaches.

For a man to live a happy life, he needs not to live by sight but by faith. Ignorance of this fact subjects man to suppression.

And because man is full of fear, he is full of negative thoughts instead of positive thoughts, which overwhelms man's subconsciousness; bad things happen in our lives instead of good. Every word of God holds, **"As a man thinketh (in his mind), so is he" - Proverbs 23:7**

Jesus came to Earth to be a role model to man, to show us how to think, reason, and live a good life full of faith. Walking on the sea is not voodoo; it is the state and condition of the mind. No wonder the bible tells us in **Hebrews 11:6. "Without faith, it is impossible to please God…"**

Hold on! Guess what? I want to highlight faith.

Reasoning and thinking emanating from man's conscious intellectual part contributes to faith. Before the foundation of our whole universe, God thought about it. For instance, when God was about to form man, he considered fashioning man into his image. So also, faith develops from the conscious state of mind to the subconscious state of the mind. That is to say, when a man thinks and reasons towards a sure thing, he desires it in his conscious state of mind; He keeps meditating upon it until it sieves into the sub-consciousness state of mind, and then it works. Jesus, our teacher, and Rabbi, tells us in the Gospel of Mark 11:24(He says:

> **"Therefore, I say unto you, what things soever ye <u>desire</u>,**
> **When ye pray, <u>believe</u> that ye receive them and shall have them."**
>
> -Mark 11:24

In this scriptural text above, one can follow the principles of faith, which is the state of mind; the principle that you have to desire it, which means thinking about it, reasoning towards it in the conscious mind (desire), which then assimilates gradually into the sub-conscious mind (i.e. believing) and then action follows; (because work done = force x distance); hence, one can say that, power is the resultant force of faith. However, faith without work is dead – (**James 2:26**)

Summarizing the statement of Jesus in Mark 11:24

❖ When one <u>desires,</u> this means thinking and reasoning in the conscious state of the mastermind.

❖ This means those thoughts and feelings assimilate with time to the sub-conscious state of the mastermind.

❖ Then, the subconscious nature makes you work as a spirit, which man is, and the action takes place. There is no limit in the spiritual realm.

All these processes are of faith. The resultant force of this faith is called POWER. Power is the dynamic ability to cause changes. Hence, Faith equals Power as Work done = Force x Distance (applying physics terms), and the mind being the willpower of man, one can say that Faith, which is the state of mind, is also the willpower of man, which results in actions.

In other words, faith is power, and power is faith; if well put, power is the resultant force of faith.

> **"For verily I say unto you, that whosoever shall say unto this mountain, be thou removed and be thou cast into the sea; and shall not doubt in his heart (MIND) but shall believe (FAITH) that those things which he saith shall come to pass, he shall have whatsoever he saith. Therefore, I say unto you, what things soever ye <u>desire</u> when you <u>pray,</u> <u>believe</u> that you receive them, and you shall have them."**
>
> **-Mark 11:23-24**

Chapter TEN

THE THREE TYPES OF SPIRIT IN THIS WORLD

In today's secular world, spirits comprise the whole universe, followed by matter. When I say matter, I am talking about any substance that has weight and occupies space. God is spirit; Man is spirit; Angels are spirits; demons are spirits; spirit here, spirit there; the universe is full of spirit beings. You can witness what I am talking about if you have a spiritual eye.

There is much warfare in the spiritual realm, even starting from heaven **(Rev. 12:7-12)**, and violence everywhere, even from the birth of John the Baptist **(Mathew 11:12)**. In the bible, St Paul, who used to say, "I know of a man, whether in the spirit or the physical. . ." take note, this man St Paul, one of the greatest apostles; sees in the spirit and he declares in Ephesians 6:12, knowing, there are spirits everywhere he forewarned us saying . . .

> **"For we wrestle not against flesh and blood, but against principalities,**
> **against powers, against the rulers of the darkness of this world,**
> **against spiritual wickedness in high places."**
>
> **-Ephesians 6:12**

There are spirits everywhere in the air (celestial kingdom), in the sea and beneath the sea (marine kingdom), on the land (terrestrial kingdom) on the mountain; in the valley, under the sea, on Mars planet, on Venus's planet; in the Bermuda triangle etc. The Biblical, practical support to this could be taken from the Book of Daniel, whereby the astral spirit by name, the Kings, and Prince of Persia, withheld the answer to the prayer of Daniel for twenty – (21) days*

It happened so drastically and dramatically that the messenger of God, Angel Gabriel, could not do anything but fight the Prince of Persia. The fight was so fierce to the extent that Archangel Michael, the chief of the cohorts of warring angels in heaven, had to come to assist Angel Gabriel. Archangel Michael was still fighting with the Prince of Persia while Angel Gabriel hastened up to deliver the message to Daniel, the prayer warrior. It took 21 days, i.e., to say the Prince of Persia withstood Angel Gabriel for 21 days, and when Archangel Michael came, he helped him. Even at that, the warfare continued in space (cloud nine), and Angel Gabriel told Daniel, the prayer warrior, I am going back to assist Archangel Michael to fight against the Prince of Persia. What a world full of Spirits and warfare.

"Then said he unto me, fear not, Daniel; for from the first day,
that thou didst set thine heart to understand and to chasten thyself before thy God,
thy words were heard, and I come for thy words. But the Prince of the Kingdom of
Persia withstood me one and twenty days, but Michael, one of the chief Princes,
came to help me, and I remain there with the Kings of Persia."

-**Daniel 10:12-13**

In verse 20, Angel Gabriel told him he was returning to assist Archangel Michael after giving Daniel the message.

"Then said he, knoweth thou wherefore I come unto thee?
And now will I return to fight with the Prince of Persia, and when I go forth,
the king of Persia shall come. But I will shew thee that which is noted
in the scripture of truth, and none holdeth with me in these things,
but Michael, your Prince."

-**Daniel 10:20-21**

Pause a little; could you perceive anything? If angels could fight, what of men who are also spirits and higher than angels and our weapon is not carnal but mighty through God (**II Cor. 10:4-6).** But ignorance is destroying man (**Hosea 4:6**). Men need to pray (**Luke 18:1).** There is power in the tongue and the in the word of a king; there is power but man, not knowing he is a spirit, and there is spiritual warfare, could not possess his possession, and it is only when man discovers this that he will recover.

Having experienced spiritual things which led to my conversion and being devotedly seeking the face of God, with fasting and prayers, I served God with great zeal. Now, out of conviction and no more out of conversion, I see many things and can tell you there is a spiritual world. Speaking about them will take about ten pages to describe. One example of this is if you are in the marine kingdom; during the day or time of the meeting, say by 24:30 hour GMT (midnight), you will get out of your body, and you will see your body lying on the bed while you have left passing through the door without unlocking it. Man is a spirit.

So, when I started worshipping God, I received many attacks; God always opened my eyes. I see things that ordinary eyes could not see; I hear voices that ordinary ear could not hear* As I walk on the road, I see demons; when they notice that I have seen them, they vanish; I see them play; I see them joined together, husband and wife, their feet not touching the ground; I see them having meetings in town halls when people have gone to sleep. I see them assembling in every road junction doing one ritual, meeting, or anything else. Some people you see move on the road; others come to buy things in the markets. Believe me, not all are human beings, and some are spirits. You see them walking as human beings with their legs, but if God opens your spiritual eyes, you will know and see some of them walking in the air; I have seen many of them, some with mirrors on their forehead. Sometimes, you might be on a bus travelling; suddenly, you will see two or three demons trying to map out an accident on the road. They can take the shape of humans or animals or stay as they exist.

Something happened one day; I have a timetable for my prayers, fasting, quiet times and other activities. So, one night, I was supposed to pray by midnight, but I felt so weak and drowsy when I woke up around 11:45 p.m. I wanted to sleep again; my flesh was weak, but I wanted to pray in my spirit. Then I was sitting on my bed, the palms of my head resting and supporting my cheek, face bent down; I was so weak. Suddenly, God opened my eyes spiritually; behold, a minor demon was under, blowing a breeze on my face. When it noticed I had seen it, it ran; then I commanded it to be blinded; all the strength in this world came upon me, and I prayed for even more than 3 hours. I could not have known such a thing was happening without God letting me know.

Many spirits are operating in this universe, as we have seen from the Bible at the beginning of this chapter. The Bible declares three types of spirit.

- The spirit of God (Holy Spirit)
- The spirit of Man (The inward and real man)
- The spirit of the world (Evil Spirit)

"⁹ But as it is written, Eye hath not seen, nor ear heard, neither have entered into the heart of man, the things which God had prepared for them that love him.

¹⁰ But God hath revealed them unto us by his spirit, for the spirit searcheth all things, yea, the deep things of God.

¹¹ For what man knoweth the things of God, save the spirit of man which is in him? Even so, the things of God knoweth no man but the spirit of God.

¹² Now we have received, not the spirit of the world, but the spirit which is of God; that we might know the things, which are freely given to us of God."

-I Corinthians 2:9-12

Henceforth, we have known there are three types of spirits, and man also is a spirit. Man living under carnality cannot understand things of the spirit which he (man) belongs to **(I Cor. 2:14)**

And because man has the willpower and virtue of knowledge of evil and good, he has the veto to control himself and rule his spirit. And the mind is the centre of the will-power of man, which could be twisted, is the discerner of man doing evil or sound, which could propel man to control his spirit and the spirit of God leading him; on the other hand; man if failed to control his God-given spirit, could be deceived by his carnality and the spirit of this world, says the spirit of evil controlling him.

"He that is slow to anger is better than the mighty; and he that ruleth his spirit than he that taketh a city."

-Proverbs 16:32

How I wish that all men could control their spirit. If they do, the seducing spirit, the spirit of the abacus (liquor), the Asmodeus spirit (spirit of fornication), incubus and succubus spirits (spirits of spiritual husband and wife), the spirit of anger, the spirit of lust, ancestral spirit etc. would not be able to possess man and control him. Let us verify what the bible says about these types of spirits in existence.

❖ In **Numbers 11:16-17**, one can visualize how God commanded Moses to assemble seventy (70) elders among the children of Israel and the spirit, which is upon Moses (the spirit of Prophecy from God, fell upon the other 70, and the assisted Moses in ministering unto the chosen race of God, the Israelites).

❖ In **Numbers 14:24**, going through from **Numbers chapter 13:26 to end**, and from **Numbers chapter 14:1-2,** one could see how the other ten spies spoke negatively to the children of Israel and caused the SPIRIT OF FEAR to possess them, and in Numbers 14:1-2, out of fear, they murmured against God. Still, among the spies, Caleb and Joshua are of a different spirit and because God promised Caleb to possess the land which he has seen because he had another spirit, and not the spirit of fear, not the spirit of timidity, but the spirit of boldness, which is of God, whereby he can cry Abba Father, and he knew that where the Spirit of God is, there is liberty **(Rom.8:15).**

"But my servant Caleb, because he had <u>another spirit with him,</u>
and hath followed me fully; him will I bring into the land whereinto
you went, and his seed shall possess it -Numbers 14:24

Other spirits that could possess man as mentioned in the bible and had been quoted of by many servants of God include…

→ Spirit of trouble (troubled spirit) – from the spirit of the world (**Gen. 41:8**)

→ Anguish Spirit (**Exodus 6:9**)

→ Jealous Spirit (**Numbers 5:14**)

→ Hardened Spirit (**Deuteronomy 2:30**)

→ Sorrowful Spirit (**I Sam1:16**)

→ Fervent Spirit (**Romans 12:11**) from God

→ God seeking Spirit (**Isaiah 26:9**) from God

→ Steadfast Spirit (**Psalm 78:8**) from God

→ Faithful Spirit (**Proverbs 11:13**) from God

→ Spirit of Wisdom (**Deuteronomy 34:9**) from God.

Hence, man must be careful; even in laying hands, there could be an impartation of some spirits; therefore, one should know who is laying hands on them and to whom they are laying hands. Some Biblical quotation has this remark for us to understand.

Search this scripture for yourself and see how spirits can be transferred.

→ Romans 1:11

→ Leviticus 4:15

→ I Timothy 5:22

→ 2 Timothy 1:6

→ Numbers 27:18-20

→ Deuteronomy 34:9

However, one of our brothers forewarned us to test all spirits, seeking the spirit of God to discern all spirits.

"¹ BELOVED, believe not every spirit, but try the spirits whether <u>they are of God</u>

because many false prophets have gone out into the world

(Being possessed by the spirit of the world)."

² At this moment, know ye the spirit of God; every spirit that confesseth that Jesus Christ

is come in the flesh is of God.

I John 4:1–2

Chapter ELEVEN

THE MYSTERY OF INIQUITY

The church today is engaged in spiritual warfare. One will ask, what is the church?

The church does not represent a building made by hand, not at all; the church is quantified by the people inside the building in as much as a school is just an empty building without learners/students. The church, as a magnificent building of astonishingly architectural fabrication, erected with stones, steel, and wood, designed with marble and granite, is not complete without man. No! The church is man and, in most cases, holy men. God is not interested in the building made by hand, but his interest is in man. It is expedient that men congregate and hear the word of God, I am not criticizing the gathering of brethren but trying to enlighten our minds in how God treasures man.

The reason why man does not understand that he is the church is because he (man) is living in carnality.

"But the natural man receives not the things of the spirit of God:
for they are foolishness unto him; neither can he know them,
because they are spiritually discerned."

- I Cor.2:14

God declares that man is the church; the essence of God creating man is for man to worship him. Even as we congregate and worship God and lift holy hands in our places of worship, one thing we must bear in mind is that God dwells in us because the era of the ark of God being kept in the Tabernacle, in the holy of holies, in the Sanctus Santorum, has metamorphosed. The worshipping of God must always be in spirit and in truth, even as God resides in us. **(John 4:24),** otherwise, your worship becomes vain.

[7] Hypocrites! Well, did Isaiah prophesy about you, saying:
[8] 'These people draw near to Me with their mouth and honour
Me with their lips, but their heart is far from Me.
[9] And in vain they worship Me, Teaching as doctrines the commandments of men.'"

-NKJV Bible. Matthew 15:7-9

Take note; it is still advisable to attend the gathering of brethren because the word of God says that iron sharpens iron, so a friend sharpens the countenance of his friend. After Jesus restores man to God in a relationship, by Grace, God desists from living in the temple built with the hand; He (God) and Jesus made their abode in man. (**John 14:23**).

> **"Know you not that ye are the temple of God,**
> **and that the spirit of God dwelleth in you?"**
>
> **- I Cor. 3:16**

Man is God's temple (church) and is a place of worship. A place where God dwells and is being glorified. And being an abode for God, man needs to be sanctified and clean.

> **"That he might present it to himself a glorious church, not having spot,**
> **or wrinkle, or any such thing, but it should be holy and without blemish."**
>
> **- Ephesians 5:27**

Until the church(man) stops being carnal and becomes spiritual, the church will be destroyed.

> **"To be carnally minded is death,**
> **but to be spiritually minded is life and peace."**
>
> **- Romans 8:6**

The warfare that man is engaged in is a continuous one. This warfare is between the spirit being and the carnal being of man. A man's soul (mind) is the judge or the referee. (Chapters 3 and 4). The mystery of iniquity is the greatest irony of life. They are the things that defile a man (church) without him recognizing it. The warfare between the spirit and the flesh is the most significant warfare of the church, and the ignorance of this makes it a mystery of iniquity. Because man is a spirit and lives in a body (flesh and blood), he is confused about who and whom he is. He is being ruled by what he sees and attends to it. All man's thoughts and actions justify the flesh; to him (man), it is a way of life. It is his nature. No! Man as a spirit needs to be led by the Spirit of God and in doing the spiritual things in controlling and dominating his universe.

> **"This says, I then, walk in the spirit, and you shall not fulfil the lust of the flesh.**
> **For the flesh lusteth against the spirit, and the spirits against the flesh:**
> **And these are contrary to the other: so that ye cannot do the things**
> **that you would. But if you are led of the spirit, you are not under the law.**
> **Now the works of the flesh are manifest, which are these: Adultery, fornication,**
> **uncleanness, lasciviousness, idolatry, witchcraft, hatred, variance, emulations,**
> **wrath, strife, seditions, heresies, envying, murders, drunkenness, reveling**
> **and such like. . . they which do such things shall not inherit the**
> **Kingdom of God. But the fruit of the spirit is love, joy, peace, longsuffering,**
> **gentleness, goodness, faith, meekness, temperance against such; there is no law."**
>
> **-Galatians 5:16-23**

> "Be not deceived; God is not mocked; for whatsoever a man soweth,
> He shall reap. For he that soweth to his flesh, shall of the flesh reap
> Corruption, but he that soweth to the spirit shall of the spirit reap life everlasting."
>
> - Galatians 6:7-8

All man's thoughts, the labours of man, are how to feed and enrich the flesh. Men and women think about what to eat, what to wear, what to drink, and how they fix their hair, paint their nails, and have sex without considering how to enrich the spirit. That is the trick Satan uses to deceive mankind- the lust of the flesh, the lust of the eyes, and the pride of life. No wonder Jesus gave us an example of the devices of Satan:

> **"But he answered and said, it is written, man shall not live by bread alone,**
> **but by every word that proceedeth out of the mouth of God."**
>
> - **Matthew 4:4**

In other words, Jesus emphasizes that even though man needs food for the body, man needs to be healthy as his soul prospers (3 John 2).

[2] Beloved, I pray that you may prosper in all things and be in health just as your soul prospers.

-NKJV Bible. 3 John 1:2

He should avoid carnal nature because he is a spirit, and his life is founded on the word of God. Man, as a spirit, should **destroy the works of the flesh** (The works of the flesh are not flesh itself. Your flesh is part of you. The works of the flesh are those sins that are out of carnality), destroying man's spiritual life. Immediately, man recognizes that he is a spirit and gives attention to building himself and cares less about the works of the flesh; the ignorance of living in the objective consciousness of the mastermind will leave him committing iniquities against himself. St. Paul understands (He still lives) this mystery of iniquity, the church's greatest warfare, and he confesses.

> **"For we know the law is spiritual, but I am carnal, sold under sin.**
> **For that which I do, I allow not: for what I would, that do I not; but what I hate,**
> **that do I. If I do that which I would not, I consent to the law that it is good.**
> **Now then, it is no longer I that do it, but sin that dwelleth in me.**
> **For I know that in me (that is, in my flesh) dwelleth no good thing; for to will**
> **is present with me; but how to perform that which is good I find not.**
> **I do not care for the good that I would, but the evil which I would not, that I do.**
> **Now, if I do that, I would not; there is no more I that do it, but sin that dwelleth in me.**
> **I find then a law that evil is present with me when I would do good.**
> **For I delight in the law of God after the <u>inward man.</u>**
> **But I see another law in my members, <u>warring</u> against the law of <u>my mind,</u>**
> **bringing me into captivity to the law of sin in my members.**
> **O wretched man that I am! Who shall deliver me from the body of this death?**

**I thank God through Jesus Christ our Lord. So then, <u>with the mind</u>,
I serve the law of God, but <u>with the flesh</u>, the law of sin."**

- Romans 7:14-25

According to the scripture, St. Paul's nature remained unchanged even after becoming familiar with Christ/ God. He had the exact nature before and after his encounter with Christ. As a Christian, he acknowledges resisting temptation and relying on God's grace to overcome it. This struggle is common to every individual living in ignorance today. The church at war is a severe case of our life today. Even many men of God are still fighting this war daily – The war of fleshy desires.

How did St. Paul curb his weak point and attain spiritual things? He admonishes us thus:

**"But I keep under my body and bring it into subjection, lest that by any means when
I have preached to others that I should be a castaway."**

- I Cor. 9:27

He declared a state of emergency on his body and subjected it to his spiritual enrichments.

King David suffered much spiritual warfare among his members. And the height is when he took Uriah's wife and made love to her. Why? Because of the lust of the flesh, the desires of the carnal nature of man fight against our spiritual nature. When he learnt how to fight against this mystery of iniquity, he declared...

**"Wherewithal shall a young man cleanse his way.
By taking heed to it according to thy word."**

Psalm 119:9

Another man in the warring part is Job. God sees a lot in Job before he boasts of him before Satan. A principled man, Job foresees this mystery of iniquity – the church at war and plans how to win it. He, therefore, made a covenant,

**"I made a covenant with my eyes; why should I think upon a maid?
(I.e., why then should I lust after a woman)."**

- Job 31:1

Most of the things we do are not worth doing. Yet we see ourselves doing them. Things like adultery, fornication, alcoholism, smoking, drugs, homosexualism, lesbianism . . . etc. It is time for man to subject down his body to attain spiritual things and reign with Jesus. **(Galatians 5:16-26)**

Chapter TWELVE

THE MANDATE (AUTHORITY) OF MAN

Authority reigns supreme in the spirit world. The spirits operate according to hierarchy and respect of powers, hence the attributes of kingdoms to different spiritual realms. Man as a spirit has a mandate from God if he (man) aligns his resonance to the frequency of God and fraternizes with divinity. Recall the case of the seven sons of Sceva in **Acts of the Apostles, chapter 19: 13-16.**

[13]Then some of the itinerant Jewish exorcists took it upon themselves to call the name of the Lord Jesus over those who had evil spirits, saying, <u>"We exorcise you by the Jesus whom Paul preaches."</u>
[14]Also, there were <u>seven sons of Sceva</u>, a Jewish chief priest, who did so.
[15]And the evil spirit answered and said, <u>"Jesus I know, and Paul I know; but who are you?"</u>
[16]Then the man in whom the evil spirit dwells leapt on them, overpowered them and prevailed against them so that they fled out of that house naked and wounded.
Acts 19:13-16 NKJV Bible.

"Jesus, I know, and Paul, I know, but who are you?"

In other words, on whose authority are you operating? Prayer and deliverance surpass speaking ordinary words. It is a spiritual exercise with a mandate. The sons of Sceva did not function with the mandate. They forgot that man's true nature is spirit and decided to work in the flesh. And as a spirit, you need to link your root to your source from where your authority emanates from.

[1]I will lift my eyes to the hills— From whence comes my help?
[2] My help comes from the Lord, who made heaven and earth.
Psalm 12 NKJV Bible.

Let us take our bible reference from Genesis chapter one, verses 26-28, to itemize the duty of man and his mandate (Authority).

[26]Then God said, "Let Us make man in Our image, according to Our likeness; let them have <u>dominion over the fish of the sea, over the birds of the air, and over the cattle, over all the earth and over every creeping thing that creeps on the earth."</u>
[27]So God created man in His own image; in the image of God He created him; male and female He created them.
[28]Then God blessed them, and God said to them, "Be fruitful and multiply; fill the earth and subdue it; <u>have dominion over the fish of the sea, over the birds of the air, and over every living thing that moves on the earth."</u>

Genesis 1:26-28 NKJV Bible.

God gave birth to man and commanded him to have dominion over the **astral, marine, and terrestrial kingdoms.** He symbolizes these domains with the fish of the sea, birds of the air, cattle and creeping things of the earth. He charged man to be fruitful, multiply, fill and subdue the earth.

However, the Levithan hoodwinked man, and he (man) was derailed by disobedience. His place and position were taken from him by Lucifer, the Leviathan. Then God came to his rescue by bringing a Godhead in human form bearing the name Jesus. In other words, God transformed into a man and came to the universe. And Jesus did not waste any time in declaring his intention and motto, having known the intention of Satan, the Leviathan and Lucifer. And he stated…

[10] The thief does not come except to steal, and to kill, and to destroy. I have come that they may have life and that they may have it more abundantly.

John 10:10 NKJV Bible.

[8] He who sins is of the devil, for the devil has sinned from the beginning. For this purpose, the Son of God was manifested that He might destroy the works of the devil.

1 John 3:8 NKJV Bible.

And now the authority, mandate, and power were taken up by Jesus from Hades after destroying the kingdom of Satan, triumphing over principalities and powers.

[10]and you are complete in Him, who is the head of all principality and power. Not Legalism but Christ
[11]In Him, you were also circumcised with the circumcision made without hands, by putting off the body of the sins of the flesh, by the circumcision of Christ,
[12]buried with Him in baptism, in which you also were raised with Him through faith in the working of God, who raised Him from the dead.
[13]And you, being dead in your trespasses and the uncircumcision of your flesh, He has made alive together with Him, having forgiven you all trespasses,

[14]having wiped out the handwriting of requirements that was against us, which was contrary to us. And He has taken it out of the way, having nailed it to the cross.
[15] Having disarmed principalities and powers, He made a public spectacle of them, triumphing over them in it.

Colossians 2:10-15 NKJV Bible.

The mandate was returned and is free for a grab but with a condition because man took what was freely given to him for granted. Let us understand this reason from the scripture below.

[1]In the beginning was the Word, and the Word was with God, and the Word was God.
[2]He was in the beginning with God.
[3]All things were made through Him, and without Him, nothing was made that was made.
[4]In Him was life, and the life was the light of men.
[5]And the light shines in the darkness, and the darkness did not and does not comprehend it.
[9]That was the true Light which gives light to every man coming into the world.
[10]He was in the world, and the world was made through Him, and the world did not know Him.
[11]He came to His own, and His own did not receive Him.
[12]But as many as received Him, to them He gave the right to become children of God, to those who believe in His name:
[13]who were born, not of blood, nor of the will of the flesh, nor of the will of man, but of God.
[14]And the Word became flesh and dwelt among us, and we beheld His glory, the glory as of the only begotten of the Father, full of grace and truth.
[16]And of His fullness, we have all received, and grace for grace.
[17]For the law was given through Moses, but grace and truth came through Jesus Christ.
[18]No one has seen God at any time. The only begotten Son, who is in the bosom of the Father, He has declared Him.

John 1:1-5,9-14,16-18 NKJV Bible

Jesus, who is and proceeded from Abba father, came to restore us back to our dignity, but we could not comprehend and accept this mystery; hence, we connived with Satan to kill him without diagnosing it was God's strategic plan to rescue mankind.

[10] He was in the world, and the world was made through Him, and the world did not know Him.
[11] He came to His own, and His own did not receive Him.

And we forsook Him, not acknowledging that Jesus is the way, the truth and life. In Him, we move; in Him, we live and have our being.
[4] In Him was life, and the life was the light of men.

[5]And the light shines in the darkness, and the darkness did not comprehend it.
[9] That was the true Light which gives light to every man coming into the world.

Here is the condition to function with Authority and have the privilege to be a son and to call Abba father, and your voice will be heard. One condition. Accepting Jesus and being guided by the Holy Spirit.

[12]Therefore, brethren, we are debtors—not to the flesh, to live according to the flesh.
[13]For if you live according to the flesh, you will die; but if by the
Spirit you put to death the deeds of the body, you will live.
[14]For as many as are led by the Spirit of God, these are sons of God.
[15]For you did not receive the spirit of bondage again to fear, but you
received the Spirit of adoption by whom we cry out, "Abba, Father."
[16]The Spirit Himself bears witness with our spirit that we are children of God,
[17]and if children, then heirs—heirs of God and joint heirs with Christ, if
indeed we suffer with Him, that we may also be glorified together.
Romans 8:12-17 NKJV Bible.

SECRET OF ACQUIRING THE MANDATE

You must be a child of God to exercise kingdom right. And this will be activated by you being born-again.

[12] But as many as received Him, to them He gave the right to become children (sons/daughters) of God, to those who believe in His name:

John 1:12

For this to be activated, man must be born again.

[3] Jesus answered and said to him, "Most assuredly, I say to you, unless
one is born again, he cannot see the kingdom of God."
John 3:3 NKJV Bible.

For you to have authority once again, to operate with a mandate, to be a son/daughter, and for daddy-God to hear you, you must be born again.

To be born again is a spiritual exercise. It is a mystery whereby the Holy Spirit will conceive you and give birth to you. Your life will no longer depend on the blood in your flesh but on the word of God.

[13] who were born, not of blood, nor of the will of the flesh, nor of the will of man, but of God.

John 1:13

God will make his abode with you, Jesus will be your companion, and Holy Spirit will always work with you. The trinity will tabernacle in you. And you will become a moving ark of God.

[4] You are of God, little children, and have overcome them because

He who is in you is greater than he who is in the world.

1 John 4:4 NKJV Bible

[26] the mystery which has been hidden from ages and from generations, but now has been revealed to His saints.

[27] To them God willed to make known what the riches of the glory of this mystery among the Gentiles are: <u>which is Christ in you, the hope of glory.</u>

Colossians 1:26-27 NKJV Bible.

This is that stage whereby you accept the finished work of God, knowing that Jesus died for you in exchange. You are ingrafted in him that while on the cross, you were there with him, buried with him, resurrected with him, and sitting with him in the heavenly places.

[4]But God, who is rich in mercy, because of His great love with which He loved us,

[5]<u>even when we were dead in trespasses, made us alive together</u>

<u>with Christ (by grace you have been saved),</u>

[6]<u>and raised us up together, and made us sit together in the heavenly places in Christ Jesus,</u>

[7]that in the ages to come He might show the exceeding riches of

His grace in His kindness toward us in Christ Jesus.

[8]For by grace you have been saved through faith, and that not of yourselves; it is the gift of God,

[9]not of works, lest anyone should boast.

Ephesians 2:4-9 NKJV Bible.

[17]that the God of our Lord Jesus Christ, the Father of glory, may give to

you the spirit of wisdom and revelation in the knowledge of Him,

[18]<u>the eyes of your understanding being enlightened; that you may know what is the</u>

<u>hope of His calling, what are the riches of the glory of His inheritance in the saints,</u>

[19]<u>and what is the exceeding greatness of His power toward us who</u>

<u>believe, according to the working of His mighty power</u>

[20]<u>which He worked in Christ when He raised Him from the dead</u>

<u>and seated Him at His right hand in the heavenly places,</u>

[21]<u>far above all principality and power and might and dominion, and every</u>

<u>name that is named, not only in this age but also in that which is to come.</u>

[22]<u>And He put all things under His feet, and gave Him to be head over all things to the church,</u>

[23]<u>which is His body, the fullness of Him who fills all in all.</u>

Ephesians 1:17-23 NKJV Bible.

Once you are born again by faith and work of grace, your sin is forgiven, and you are raised to reign with Jesus in the heavenly places. You will be operating above principalities and powers. Your voice can ascend and penetrate realms. You will have power and dominion and authority. You will be more than a conqueror; God will make you rule over your enemies and have dominion. In this way, the mandate is restored.

[1] The Lord said to my Lord, "Sit at My right hand, Till I make Your enemies Your footstool."
[2] The Lord shall send the rod of Your strength out of Zion. Rule thou in the midst of Your enemies!

Psalms 110:1-2 NKJV Bible.

Chapter THIRTEEN

VOICES THAT TRANSCEND THE BARRIERS OF REALMS.

Speeches of ordinary men are mere words that circulate the four walls of our vicinity. When sons speak, even the sun hears and obeys, as recorded in Joshua 10:1-15. The voice of the sons of God, men with mandate, controls both animate and inanimate objects. Even the spirits, demons, dominions, thrones, kingdoms, principalities, and powers hear them and obey. More also is the blood of the innocent, as recorded in Genesis 4:10.

Why is it so? The ultimate reason is that man is a spirit, and if such a man is holy, no barrier can withstand him. This means that their voices are quickened by the Holy Spirit and are full of divine energy to penetrate barriers, and there is life in them because anything spirit cannot be inactive and lifeless.

> **[63] It is the Spirit who gives life; the flesh profits nothing. <u>The words that I speak to you are spirit, and they are life.</u>**
>
> **John 6:63 NKJV Bible.**

A man with a mandate is not ordinary. He has the capacity to transcend realms. His voice transcends, his words are spirits, and they are life. Demons, spirits, death, dominions and thrones, sicknesses and diseases obey the voices of sons who call upon Him. Voices that transcend realms are the blood of the innocent and the voice of sons of God with mandate and authority.

The word of God, the words of mandated sons, and the blood of the innocent are respected by God. This is that voice that casts out demons, raises the dead, opens blind eyes, unstops deaf ears, and heals the sick. Man has the power to penetrate realms where captivities are operated, scatter it, and the result will be healing. Man has the capacity to go beyond realms, call back a dead person, and it will come back to life.

Abel's blood speaks, the blood of the innocent also speaks, and Jesus' blood also speaks better and louder things.

For a man to operate with a voice God cannot resist, demons and spirits will always tremble on its projections, and four things need to be put in place.

- **Consecration**
- **Fasting**
- **Prayers and**
- **Word of God**

These are the four key factors man can use to enrich his spirit. Once a man engages in these activities and prays to his father in secret, his father, who sees in secret, will reward him openly. This revelation comes directly from Jesus, our master and Lord.

> **[6] But you, when you pray, go into your room, and when you have shut your door, pray to your Father who is in the secret place; and your Father who sees in secret will reward you openly.**
>
> **Matthew 6:6 NKJV Bible.**

Man should regularly do this exercise to always ascend into realms. Once practiced, you don't need to pray once you confront issues, you only say a word. This is effective because you have already discussed matters arising with your Abba father in the secret place, your closet. As a man full of power and mandate, your words are now the words of God; your voice can now project realms and are spirits and life.

Recall the incident at the beautiful gate with Peter, John, and the lame man…

Peter and John, on meeting the lame man at the beautiful gate, did not pray for him. They only ascended into realms when they commanded him to look at them; they went where his problem was being orchestrated in the spirit realm, untied him, and came back to their physical being and said a word, '**rise up and walk**'. This word becomes spirit and life to the bones of the lame man.

> **[2]And a certain man lame from his mother's womb was carried, whom they laid daily at the gate of the temple, which is called Beautiful, to ask alms from those who entered the temple;**
> **[3]who, seeing Peter and John about to go into the temple, asked for alms.**
> **[4]And fixing his eyes on him, with John, Peter said, "Look at us."**
> **[5]So he gave them his attention, expecting to receive something from them.**
> **[6]Then Peter said, "Silver and gold I do not have, but what I do have I give you: In the name of Jesus Christ of Nazareth, rise up and walk."**
> **[7]And he took him by the right hand and lifted him up, and immediately his feet and ankle bones received strength.**
> **[8]So he, leaping up, stood and walked and entered the temple with them—walking, leaping, and praising God.**

[9]And all the people saw him walking and praising God.
[10]Then they knew that it was he who sat begging alms at the Beautiful
Gate of the temple, and they were filled with wonder and amazement at
what had happened to him. Preaching in Solomon's Portico
[11] Now, as the lame man who was healed held on to Peter and John, all the people
ran together to them on the porch, which is called Solomon's, greatly amazed.
[12] So when Peter saw it, he responded to the people: "Men of Israel, why do you marvel at this? Or
why look so intently at us, as though by our own power or godliness we had made this man walk?
[13]The God of Abraham, Isaac, and Jacob, the God of our fathers, glorified His Servant Jesus,
whom you delivered up and denied in the presence of Pilate when he was determined to let Him go.
[14]But you denied the Holy One and the Just and asked for a murderer to be granted to you,
[15]and killed the Prince of life, whom God raised from the dead, of which we are witnesses.
[16]And His name, through faith in His name, has made this man strong,
whom you see and know. Yes, the faith which comes through Him has
given him this perfect soundness in the presence of you all.

Acts 3:2-16 NKJV Bible.

When the people marvelled at what had happened, they could let them know that this is the true nature of man, if only they could recognise the power, authority and mandate they have through Jesus Christ.

[11] Now, as the lame man who was healed held on to Peter and John, all the people ran together to them on the porch, which is called Solomon's, greatly amazed.
[12] So when Peter saw it, he responded to the people: "Men of Israel, why do you marvel at this? Or why look so intently at us, as though by our own power or godliness we had made this man walk?
[13] The God of Abraham, Isaac, and Jacob, the God of our fathers, glorified His Servant Jesus….
[16] And His name, through faith in His name, has made this man strong, whom you see and know. Yes, the faith which comes through Him has given him this perfect soundness in the presence of you all.

The same applies to the raising of the dead. You do not pray to raise the dead. You call them back to life. And because you have the mandate, your voice will project to the realms of the dead and bring the dead back to life. This is the reward of sonship to Abba father. Our Lord Jesus demonstrated these when called …Lazarus, come forth when he commanded the little damsel, Talitha Cumi when he commanded deaf ear, Ephphatha!

In the case of demons and spirits, exorcism, as many preferred, you do not pray for them to go or ask God to deal with them; you cast them out with command in the name of Jesus.
You have the authority to heal, oh son of man. When will you achieve your full potential?

[17] And these signs will follow those who believe: In My name<u>, they</u> <u>will cast out demons;</u> they will speak with new tongues; . . .

Mark 16:17 NKJV Bible.

In other place, Jesus instructed the apostles.,

[1] And when He had called His twelve disciples to Him, <u>He gave them power over unclean spirits, to</u> <u>cast them out, and to heal all kinds of sickness and all kinds of disease.</u> Matthew 10:1 NKJV Bible.

This is your heritage as a son/daughter of God, of whom man is. When shall man discover himself and recover?

The whole creation is waiting for you, sons, and daughters of God!

[19] For the earnest expectation of the creation eagerly waits for the revealing of the sons of God.

Romans 8:19 NKJV Bible.

Printed in the United States
by Baker & Taylor Publisher Services